RETAIL ACCOUNTABILITY

UCLan

0 1 SEP 2011

LEARNING & INFORMATION
SERVICE

D1428579

30107 006 267 675

RETAIL ACCOUNTABILITY

Advanced Retail Profitability Analysis

STEVEN LINDNER

With Barbara A. Chernow

UC LIBRARY
NOV 12

Fairchild
Publications, Inc.

Executive Editor: Olga T. Kontzias
Assistant Acquisitions Editor: Carolyn Purcell
Art Director: Adam B. Bohannon
Director of Production: Priscilla Taguer
Development Editor: Barbara A. Chernow
Editor: Anne Chan
Assistant Production Editor: Beth Applebome
Editorial Assistant: Suzette Lam
Copy Editor: John King
Text Design: Susan Day
Cover Design: Adam B. Bohannon

Copyright © 2004
Fairchild Publications, Inc.

All rights reserved. No part of this book covered by the copyright hereon may be reproduced or used in any form or by any means—graphic, electronic, or mechanical, including photocopying, recording, taping, or information storage and retrieval systems—without written permission of the publisher.

Library of Congress Catalog Card Number: 2003113636

ISBN: 1-56367-314-2
GST R 133004424

Printed in the United States of America

6267675

UCLan

0 1 SEP 2011

LEARNING & INFORMATION
SERVICE

To my sisters, Lorin and Marilyn.
I only wish my parents were alive to share this moment.

Contents

Extended Contents

Preface

The fundamental goal of any retail business is to maximize the return on its investment. For both buyer and seller, this means earning the largest possible profit through the sale of inventory. Thus, both retailers and manufacturers must be familiar with the advanced mathematical skills necessary to create and analyze profitability reports. Such reports evaluate products bought at wholesale prices and sold at retail in terms of profitability. They measure the amount of gross margin dollars that each manufacturer or supplier contributes to a business. Gross margin dollars, which are the most accurate measurement of potential retail profit, are those dollars that exist after the retailer deducts the direct and indirect costs of the merchandise that was sold. They are used to pay all operating or fixed expenses of the business, including rent, salaries, advertising, utilities, professional fees, taxes, and insurance. Only if a business' gross margin dollars exceed operating expenses has that business earned a profit. Thus, retailers buy from those wholesalers whose products sell well enough to generate the gross margin dollars needed for profits.

Currently, no text focuses specifically on the advanced mathematical techniques required to assess profitability reports. Because a manufacturer's fate often hangs in the balance of the analysis derived from these reports, understanding each element of these reports—and their implications for future business—is essential for both buyer and seller. Because these skills are often neglected in academic programs, many professionals are trying to run businesses without these tools.

This text is designed to fill that gap. Part One focuses on the basic components of the buyer-vendor relationship, including the strengths and weaknesses of each during negotiations, the elements and calculations necessary to create and assess profitability reports, and possible areas of miscalculation because of different meanings or interpretations of specific charges and costs. Part Two explains how to interpret standard financial reports, such as profit-and-loss statements. Each chapter presents its subject in the form of explanatory text, practical examples with solutions, practice exercises, and research projects. This material is enhanced by case studies, points of view, and sidebars that provide additional background material. Part Three includes final examinations in the form of exercises and projects that cover all of the material in this text. The back of the text includes a glossary of terms, answers to odd-numbered exercises, and an index. A separate answer manual contains solutions to all exercises in the text.

Clearly, this is not a text for beginners. Students should already have basic retail mathematics skills. By the end of the text, however, students should be able to understand and check the accuracy of retail profitability reports presented in almost all formats. At the end, students should be able to complete the questions in the final examinations.

For the past ten years, I have used the techniques explained in this text at both the academic level as a teacher of retail mathematics and in the field as a consultant to such clients as Donna Karan, Calvin Klein, Escada, and Giorgio Armani. This text grew out of those experiences.

Acknowledgments

I am extremely grateful to the Fairchild family, Olga Kontzias, Carolyn Purcell, and Beth Applebome. Their collective wisdom and faith helped bring this book to fruition.

In addition, many thanks to my developmental editor, Barbara Chernow, who slaved through my hieroglyphics and tortured use of the English language to find order.

As a teacher at Parsons School of Design for more than a decade, I honed my skills in a challenging environment. I thank my colleagues and students.

Special thanks to Amy Pace and Tammey Sharpe, who had to endure my angst as I completed this book, as well as to Lisa and Kim for their corporate support. Finally, thanks to my quartet of cousins, Ira, David, Bruce, and Gil.

Reviewers selected by the publisher were very helpful in writing this book. They include Kathryn Callahan, Central Missouri State University; Tim Christiansen, Montana State University; Linda Cushman, Syracuse University; Ann Fairhurst, University of Tennessee; Karen Guthrie, Virginia Commonwealth University; Nancy J. Miller, Iowa State University; Sharon Pate, Illinois State University; Joseph Salvati, Parsons School of Design; Leslie Stoel, Ohio State University; and Scarlett Wesley, University of South Carolina.

Steven Lindner

Abbreviations

This is a list of common abbreviations that appear throughout this textbook. Definitions of these and other terms can be found in the glossary.

BOM	Beginning of month
COD	Cash on delivery
EOM	End of month
FOB	Free on board; freight on board
GM	Gross margin
GMROI	Gross margin return per dollar of inventory
IMU	Initial markup percentage
MD	Markdown
Mds	Merchandise
MMU	Maintained markup
MU	Markup
OPX	Operating expenses
OTB	Open to buy
P/L	Profit and loss
PMD	Planned markdown
ROG	Receipt of goods
TMH	Total merchandise handled

RETAIL ACCOUNTABILITY

PART ONE
Buyer-Vendor Relationships

The key to a successful retail relationship is to negotiate terms that result in a **profit** for both the buyer and the **vendor**. To achieve this goal, each side must understand how the other is defining specific terms and the different ways in which profitability can be measured. Because buyers and vendors frequently define terms differently, vendors must have a clear understanding of each buyer's use of these terms to avoid a significant financial loss and a misunderstanding that could affect future deals.

With the advent of computers, an industry that had been dominated by personal relationships between sales representatives and retail buyers has found itself governed by detailed, accurate, and up-to-the minute reports that can analyze the profitability of an entire store, a specific department, or a particular line of goods. Although personal relationships remain important, negotiations are increasingly based on a retailer's assessment of the anticipated profits; these, in turn, are based on an analysis of recent transactions with the vendor.

In negotiating a deal, buyers and vendors need to understand the different types of relationships that may exist, the give-and-take necessary for a successful partnership, how each side measures profitability, the rudiments of negotiation, the importance of **merchandise** turnover, and differences in methods of **markup**. In the end, the buyer's assessment of the amount of profit earned from a vendor's product is summed up in the Retailer's Report Card, which is the single most important factor in determining future deals.

CHAPTER 1 / Types of Relationships

When most individuals hear the term "vendor," they envision the umbrella-covered frankfurter stand on the corners of major American cities. However, retailers use the term to describe all their product suppliers. Even the most famous manufacturers, such as Louis Vuitton, Donna Karan, and Rolls Royce, are considered vendors by the retail stores to which they sell.

Retailers began using professional buyers during the prosperous 1920s. From then, through the Great Depression, and into the late 1970s, buyer-vendor relationships were fairly straightforward. The store buyer placed orders for all kinds of merchandise. As long as the retailer shipped the product as it was originally purchased by the buyer, the transaction was complete. If the product purchased did not "retail well" (i.e., produce enough sales), the retailer would do no further business with that supplier and would search the market for a new product supplier.

At that time, retail stores had no computers and determining profitability was still an inexact process. Buyers worked with statistics and selling reports that were computed by hand and were often inaccurate. Sometimes, a buyer could only determine which items were the "fast" or "slow" sellers. All other merchandise fell into a gray area; these items were just marked down and never showed up in any useful report for analysis. Thus, relationships between buyers and vendors were based on personality and grew stronger as long as the sales stayed on track. Buyers were showered with gifts, tickets to Broadway shows, limousines, and lavish dinners. When presenting new lines, manufacturers held extravagant parties. It was, some said, like "show business," but all that was about to change.

In today's electronically controlled, immediate data-access environment, relationships are based largely on profitability. Each retailer is expected to establish objectives or plans that detail the amount of profit each supplier or manufacturer must provide to meet overall profitability goals. Because computers provide access to a vast

GONE WITH THE WIND

With the end of World War I, the United States enjoyed new heights of prosperity and optimism. In the 1920s, every sector of the economy, including **retailing**, transportation, entertainment, and housing thrived and profits on the stock market seemed limitless. Although retail stores had existed before then, the retail industry really burst into existence during this decade with a significant expansion of both department stores and small specialty shops. As a result of this increased competition, major U.S. cities were able to offer customers a wider variety of products. The success of such retail stores also created opportunities for large and small entrepreneurs to open their own businesses. In fact, some retail outlets became so successful that owners began to hire professional buyers to find the best products at the best prices for their consumers.

Such prosperity, however, could not continue forever. On Halloween, October 31, 1929, during what is now known as "Black Friday," the stock market crashed, and millions of dollars were lost in a matter of seconds. As news spread, people panicked and raced to withdraw their savings from banks. But because banks only keep a small fraction of their deposits on hand, they ran out of cash. This "run on the banks" broke the hearts and destroyed the confidence of many Americans, who lost their entire savings. The causes of the crash are generally accepted as overproduction of goods, curtailment of foreign markets after World War I, and easy money policies that led to overexpansion of credit and speculation in stocks. During the 1930s, as much as one-third of the U.S. labor force was unemployed.

Gone were the days of prosperity. The Great Depression had arrived.

array of instant information that accurately monitors every facet of a store's operation, buyers of each department or product classification are routinely and regularly kept informed of profitability figures. Every supplier to a retailer, regardless of product type, is measured by profitability.

Therefore, much as a child in grade school anxiously awaits a report card, each manufacturer anxiously awaits a "Retailer's Report Card," because that report card will often determine the fate of the supplier. The key is whether the retailer achieved its planned **gross margin** (GM) percentage or if the retailer had a difficult time "moving" or "selling" the product to disinterested consumers.

The fact is that a manufacturer must produce enough gross margin dollars each and every season for its retail customers if it wants to be assured of a continuing relationship. If the supplier fails to meet the established standard of profitability, tough negotiations with the retailer will follow. Because these often include requests by the retailer for monetary compensation for losses if the relationship is to continue, manufacturers spend millions of potential profit dollars to repair unsuccessful productivity levels.

TYPES OF RELATIONSHIPS

There are as many possible scenarios for buyer-vendor relationships as there are personality types. The following four probably account for 90 percent of the possibilities: (1) solicitation, (2) casual-informal/sporadic, (3) mutual need, and (4) confrontational.

Solicitation

Manufacturers of all products are always interested in adding new accounts (e.g., retailers, catalogs, Internet) to their client lists. Thus, the first step in any relationship is the introduction of the vendor to the buyer. When an account representative first calls on a possible new account, it is called "cold calling." Even if the retail buyer declines an invitation to view the supplier's product line, the supplier should always keep the door open for future business by remaining friendly. People frequently change positions, an existing

REVOLVING DOOR POLICY

Many large retail conglomerates have the influence to make some very strong demands of their suppliers (manufacturers). One common request is the right to return any merchandise that fails to sell in their stores. This arrangement for buying and returning product is known as the "revolving door policy." If manufacturers do not agree to such a policy, they can lose the account. If they do agree and sales are unexpectedly low, their profits can be lost as merchandise comes storming back for credit.

supplier may suddenly fall out of favor, and buyers can have excellent memories. One never knows when a closed door will open.

During the initial presentation to the retailer, the manufacturer's salesperson will explain why the retailer cannot exist without the product. If the retailer decides to buy some product, ground rules need to be established. The key issues that should be considered before entering into any **purchase order** contract are:

1. **Terms of sale,** discounts, dating, etc.
2. Terms of payment for freight
3. Return policy for:
    a. Damaged products
    b. Slow sellers
4. **Charge backs** for such vendor mistakes as:
    a. **Purchase order violations**
    b. **Routing violations**
    c. **Workroom costs**

In addition, the follow items should be discussed if the vendor and buyer enter into a "profitability contract":

1. Terms of payment for shortages and employee discounts
2. Markdown dollar allowance
3. Guaranteed gross margin

Manufacturers can become concerned by the number of violations and other costs inherent in dealing with particular retailers that expect to be protected from loss by having the manufacturer guarantee a specific profit margin. See Chapter 2 for additional information on entering into a partnership account.

Casual-Informal/Sporadic

Casual relationships begin during the solicitation stage and last until either the buyer or vendor (or both) have reached such a point in **sales volume** dollars that a dependency is created. When a retailer or manufacturer recognizes that the other is necessary to meet

ON THE ROAD

Although hundreds of retailers have merged into a handful of retail giants, thousands of small, independent mom-and-pop stores exist. These stores usually make their purchases at "shows" or from roadmen. Depending on the type of merchandise carried, the retailer usually has a variety of events to attend. For example, in men's sportswear, there was an average of one show per month slated for the year 2002 alone.

To augment purchases made at these shows, retailers purchase from traveling salespeople, such as the anachronistic "roadman." These hard-working, tediously driving, valise-displaying, mobile individuals travel the same routes year in and year out. They have one distinct advantage in working with small retailers—the owners of the businesses are also the buyers. Most major retailers, for example, change buyers on average every three years. Thus, just when a relationship becomes established, the showroom salesperson gets a new buyer. In contrast, the relationship between the roadman and store owners can last twenty years. The roadman becomes part of the retailer's family.

The obvious advantages of these close, long-range relationships are easy to comprehend. Roadmen usually carry numerous product lines from various manufacturers. So, even if a retailer does not do well with one product, the roadman generally has another product to offer. As a result of this extensive arsenal of original merchandise, the roadman can usually overcome the retailer's disapproval of some of his merchandise.

sales goals, the relationship will move to the next—mutual need—level.

The casual relationship can, however, last for years, during which both parties, while pleased with one another, do not develop a dependence. The retailer simply does not make sufficiently large purchases for that manufacturer to become a "key" supplier. If a manufacturer realizes that a retailer will never become a significant account, all sense of urgency is lost.

Mutual Need

With time, the retailer may place such a significantly large purchase with a manufacturer that the retailer's success depends on receiving and selling that product. As a rule of thumb, this occurs if a retailer places 15 percent or more of a season's opening budget with a manufacturer. If anything interferes with meeting those goals, such as the manufacturer's failure to ship the entire order, the retailer will have a difficult time meeting sales expectations. Thus, as the volume of business increases, both the retailer and manufacturer grow dependent on one another for mutual profits. Such a relationship can last indefinitely, with the manufacturer obviously trying to gain more and more floor space as long as profits escalate. To better match their products to their customers, many manufacturers display their goods in showrooms that try to anticipate the needs of buyers.

Confrontational

At what point does a mutually beneficial relationship become a confrontational one? Normally, one of two events can cause a great relationship to deteriorate. The first is when the retailer has not sold the manufacturer's product to the extent expected. The retailer's profitability will suffer and negotiations become necessary to address the issue. If any prearranged deals were made to cover such a contingency, the negotiations will be based on established parameters. If, however, the retailer has one or more poor performance (i.e., no profit) seasons and the contract did not include any preset deal to cover such a contingency, skilled negotiations become necessary. If

INSIDE SCOOP

Relationships: A Key Factor in the Success of a Business

Denise Caruso

Denise Caruso heads her own consulting firm, Pop Concepts, which specializes in public relations and marketing strategies.

THE BUSINESS

Couture Café was a wholesale accessory showroom on Fifth Avenue in New York City that presented 25 different collections from young and upcoming designers in several categories, including millinery, handbags, scarves, hair accessories, and fine and costume jewelry. The showroom displayed the collections to wholesale buyers and press from around the world, took orders on the merchandise, and forwarded those orders to the designers or manufacturers, who produced the order and shipped the merchandise to the retail outlet by the predetermined date.

DESIGNERS/MANUFACTURERS

For designers and manufacturers, who need sellable, well-priced and well-focused collections, the showroom helps by providing information about trends in the marketplace and feedback on current collections. Because manufacturers may not be geographically close to the showroom, they can become isolated from the fashion pulse of New York. Thus, the showroom is often the manufacturer's sole contact with the wholesale marketplace.

WHOLESALE BUYERS

Most showrooms work with specialty boutiques, department stores, and catalog companies. The showroom must anticipate the different needs of each type of buyer, especially since today, buying is a numbers game. The showroom staff must be aware of the stress buyers face when ordering for the season. A buyer's job is only as secure as the last successful purchases. Every season, the items they purchase must have a good sell through. They have to make buys that keep the merchandise fresh knowing that their jobs are at risk if a product does not sell.

A good showroom knows the retail outlet and can suggest appropriate merchandise. If the staff convinces a buyer to take a chance on a product and that product does not sell, the buyer will look for new sources for future purchases, so such recommendations should focus on the seller's needs.

the negotiations are successful, no interruption of business may occur.

The second is when the manufacturer grows concerned about the amount of charge backs, which often take place without the manufacturer's knowledge. For example, a manufacturer may be anticipating a payment of $20,000 from a retailer, but the accounting office receives a check for only $16,000. The other $4,000 disappeared in a list of deductions taken by the retailer to cover the costs of routing violations, purchase order violations, damaged goods given to charities, and/or **markdown allowances**.

Charge backs from retailers are a major contributor to the development of confrontational relationships. Often, manufacturers see their profits significantly diminish or disappear because of these charges. Such a relationship makes it difficult to operate in a mutually profitable environment, although negotiations may resolve the difficulties.

TERMS OF SALE

As an example of one of the key points in negotiations between buyers and vendors, the various terms of sale are discussed below. As a general rule, if no terms of sale are expressed, a retailer has 30 days to pay an invoice **(net payment date)**; no discounts are permitted. However, a purchase order may include any of the following **dating** provisions. Both the buyer and manufacturer must be clear about these terms before finalizing a sale.

Net payment: Terms of sale listed, as net means that no discounts may be taken.

4/10 net 30 or (4/10): Terms expressed in this manner allow a retailer to take a 4 percent discount on the billed **cost** of merchandise, if the retailer pays the **invoice** within 10 days of the invoice date. If the retailer does not pay within 10 days, no discount is given. The retailer has 20 days after the passing of the **discount date** in which to pay the invoice at net. This means the retailer has 30 days from the invoice date to pay the retailer with no discount.

ROG (receipt of goods) dating: Receipt of goods dating changes the payment due date from the date on the invoice to the date on which the retailer received the merchandise. Keep in mind that invoices and merchandise are not necessarily shipped the same day, or even from the same part of the country.

COD (cash on delivery) dating: When a retail store is new or has a poor credit rating, vendors may require full payment of the invoice when the merchandise is received. Although the term COD specifies cash, a business check is usually an acceptable form of payment.

EOM (end of month) dating: This means one of two different payment schedules depending on the day of the month on the invoice. The first is for invoices dated from the 1st to the 24th of a month. An invoice dated June 10, for example, with the terms 8/10 EOM, means an 8 percent discount is given if the retailer pays the invoice ten days after the end of the month—in this case, July 10. An invoice dated May 17 with the terms 5/10 EOM would give the retailer until June 10 to pay and still receive a 5 percent discount. Remember this means ten days from the end of the month in the invoice date.

The second payment schedule is for invoices dated from the 25th day of the month until the last day of the month. For example, an invoice is dated March 25 with the terms 5/10 EOM. In this case, the retailer does not have to pay ten days from the end of March to receive the discount, but rather ten days from the end of the following month. Thus, in this case, the March 25 invoice can be paid as late as May 10—and still include the discount.

With EOM dating, retailers who do not pay by the discount date have 20 days from that date to pay the invoice without receiving the discount.

Extra dating: This simply allows extra time for a retailer to pay an invoice by either the discount or net date. Usually a store receives terms as follows:

$$4/10 + 30X$$

This means the retailer has 40 days, instead of the usual 10 days, to receive the discount or 60 days to pay without the discount.

FOB (free on board; freight on board): The FOB terms establish both the legal transfer of ownership of the goods from the manufacturer to the retailer and also the point at which the retailer pays the cost of freight. For example:

FOB factory: This specifies transfer of ownership and freight costs from the factory or warehouse. Thus, the retailer owns the goods and pays for the freight at the point of shipment from the vendor.

FOB store: This specifies that the manufacturer pays all freight and has full ownership of the merchandise until delivery to the retailer.

SUMMARY

As with all types of relationships, the buyer-vendor relationship is affected by personalities. Remember, this is business, and decisions should not be made or taken personally. Salespeople should not take offense when a business relationship enters a tough patch and the retailer becomes somewhat dismissive. Keep working at accomplishing your goals by establishing a mutually profitable relationship.

EXERCISES

1. Explain how the four steps or levels of buyer-vendor relationships can be viewed as "an evolutionary process" that should not have to reach the fourth stage.

2. Some retail stores make the manufacturer pay for its own employees' discounts when a manufacturer's product is sold to one of the retailer's employees. Explain the moral and ethical considerations at work in this arrangement.

3. Explain why a retail store might request that a vendor guarantee a certain amount of sales or profits.

4. Explain why the FOB location is of paramount importance.

5. If a purchase order reads, "FOB Bombay India," are shipping costs included in the cost price?

6. Explain ROG dating.

7. If an invoice was dated March 10, 2002 and had terms of 8/10 EOM, what is the last day the invoice can be paid and still receive the 8 percent discount?

8. If an invoice is dated June 27 and has terms of 8/10 EOM, what is the last date the invoice can be paid and still receive the 8 percent discount?

9. If a buyer fails to specify terms of sale, and the manufacturer has no predetermined terms, how long would it take for the manufacturer's invoice to be paid, and what would be the discount?

10. What is meant by "net terms"?

11. What is meant by "COD dating"?

12. If an invoice is dated May 10 and has terms of sale of 4/10 + 30X, what is the last day the invoice can be paid and still receive the 4 percent discount?

13. Why should a retailer always try to have freight "prepaid"?

14. Complete the following chart:

	Terms	Invoice Date	Goods in Store	Last Date for Discount	Last Date for Payment
I.	No terms	April 2	April 4	a)	b)
II.	Net 10	April 8	April 10	a)	b)
III.	4/10	June 25	June 29	a)	b)
IV.	ROG 2/10	June 10	June 16	a)	b)
V.	5/10 EOM	May 29	May 31	a)	b)
VI.	4/10 + 30X	June 10	June 12	a)	b)

PROJECTS

1. Buyers needed to cancel product on order to bring stock levels into line. Discuss the issues involved when a buyer cancels a purchase order. Remember that a purchase order is, in fact, a contract. Your discussion should also consider the ramifications of a manufacturer's decision to sue the retailer that decides to cancel an order for merchandise that was purchased, but not yet due to ship to the retailer. Research the historical precedents for such purchase order cancellations.

2. The class will be divided into four groups. One of the four possible buyer-vendor relationships will be assigned to each group. Each group will then subdivide into vendors and retailers and complete the following exercises.

   a. Last spring, unprecedented cold weather across the nation resulted in huge losses for retailers. Write a description of the next meeting between the retailer and the vendor. Keep in mind the goals of each party. The retailer needs to minimize the loss from huge inventories of "out-of-season" stock, while the manufacturer is hoping for new purchase orders.

   b. The buyer for a nationwide chain of housewares specialty stores is facing a dilemma. Because of the closing of many of its branches, the chain is now considerably overbought and must cancel substantial quantities of "on-order" merchandise. Describe how the buyer goes about canceling these orders in each of the possible relationships. For example, buyer tactics and attitudes might be considerably different in a "casual relationship" than in one of "mutual need."

CHAPTER 2 / Deals: The Intricacies of Partnership

On the most basic level, buying a product to sell at a profit seems straightforward and elementary. The roles and objectives of all parties are clearly defined. What began centuries ago in the form of bartering has evolved into the formal retailing process that now exists.

Because the underlying principle seems so basic, newcomers to the field may assume that the process is uncomplicated. You simply purchase merchandise and sell as much as possible at the highest price the consumer is willing to pay.

In reality, however, the relationship is not so simple. The neophyte retailer quickly learns that every purchase must produce enough gross margin dollars to contribute toward **operating expenses** as well as produce a profit. Every sale of a product can be assigned a measure of profitability. By using the principles explained in this text, the retailer can calculate the predicted gross margin dollars that will be earned on a purchase even before it is received and put on sale. Problems arise when the retailer judges a manufacturer's performance or "sell through" to be unsatisfactory. Because gross margin dollars create all profits, GM calculation is the most carefully monitored calculation in retail mathematics.

Deals are structured to ensure the retailer that purchases from a given manufacturer will be protected. Thus, manufacturers guarantee that if their products are not profitable, they will cover the shortfall in gross margin dollars. These shortfall dollars are known as markdown dollars. With these assurances, the retailer can now make purchases with confidence.

The manufacturer's imperative in negotiating a fair and balanced deal is always to consider how each retailer formulates "gross margin." In the simplest sense, **gross margin** is defined as **net sales** minus the cost of merchandise sold. Usually, the cost of merchandise sold is the actual cost of merchandise minus trade discounts plus freight costs. However, many retailers also include other costs in their gross margin calculation, such as workroom costs, employee discounts, and shortages. The manufacturer is responsible for asking each retailer to itemize these costs before guaranteeing a gross margin. Otherwise, a manufacturer will be surprised to discover that after a comparison of actual versus planned gross margin, his calculation of gross margin differs greatly from that of the retailer.

For example, a manufacturer and retailer agree to a gross margin guarantee of 40 percent. At the conclusion of the selling period the manufacturer calculates gross margin as follows:

Net sales	$100,000	
− Total cost	$ 60,000	
GM	$ 40,000	(40%)

Thus, the manufacturer believes the gross margin guarantee has been met.

The retailer, however, calculates the gross margin as follows:

GM	40%
− Shortages	2%
− Employee discounts	2%
Actual GM	36%

According to this calculation, the manufacturer needs to make up for a 4 percent shortfall. Clearly, the manufacturer's calculation did not include all of the costs included in the retailer's calculation.

With this information, the manufacturer can negotiate a more realistic deal, so that the gross margin is not eroded by unexpected costs. Because gross margin dollars are the key to a retailer's success, the issue of covering shortfalls can make or break a deal. Such deals can be established before or after the actual purchases of products.

COMPONENTS OF A DEAL

In negotiating with a manufacturer, the retailer's goal is to construct a deal that protects its gross margin needs if the product does not sell well to the consumer. To achieve this goal, the retailer has an impressive arsenal at its disposal.

The manufacturer, in turn, will concede only as much as is dictated by the retailer's potential to offer huge sales volume. Thus, the smaller retailer and neighborhood specialty stores can offer relatively few incentives for manufacturers to improve the deal. A skilled negotiator, however, may still be able to secure some concessions from a manufacturer.

Retailer's Bargaining Chips

In negotiating a deal, the retailer brings the following incentives to the table:

1. The promise of current and/or continuing purchases, with potential for a significant sales increase for the manufacturer;
2. The promise of key placement for best exposure of the product in the store;
3. The promise of placement in many "doors." (An individual retail store in a chain is considered a "door.")

Options

As negotiations proceed, the following options are usually on the table:

1. A guaranteed gross margin by the manufacturer;
2. A program that allows the retailer to return merchandise that does not sell;
3. Special purchases for the retailer to help gross margin cover off-price merchandise.

In addition, almost all major retailers have one or more of these implicit requirements when placing an order with a manufacturer. If your store does not include the following vendor requirements as standard policy, consider negotiating them as additional requests:

HOLDUP OF PAYMENT

Many retailers will not pay a new vendor's invoices until the buyer gives authorization to the accounting department. This procedure protects the retailer from any complications inherent in the new manufacturer's product. For instance, if a retail buyer feels that the product received is not compatible to the samples from which the buyer placed her order, payment will be held up. This restriction or "holdup" of payment, which is often known as a "buyer's hold on payment," can last for months. Even if the invoice is "past due" by several months, release of the buyer hold must be orchestrated.

Knowledge of this procedure is important to the often unsuspecting manufacturer, who may be in dire need of funds to conduct business. The manufacturer often has to call the buyer and have this hold released for payment to be released. For the manufacturer who sells to a retailer for the first time, the topic of holdup on payments should be discussed.

FACTORING

Some manufacturers use a special kind of bank that has no tellers, no cash, and no toaster giveaways as a way to raise short-term funds. These banks and bankers are known as commercial finance companies, or factors.

The business of factoring is more than five hundred years old. When factors were first established, farmers would put up collateral—their home, barn, or livestock—to borrow money. Today, a manufacturer "sells" an outstanding invoice to the factor at a discount and then borrows money against the invoice. As a result of this arrangement, the manufacturer raises immediate cash, is relieved of the task of collecting payments, and minimizes its record keeping. After the factor has purchased the invoices, the retailer is instructed to make payment directly to the factor rather than to the manufacturer from whom the goods were purchased.

Freight considerations;

Trade or other "discounts" on all purchases;

"Extra dating" (additional time given to the retailer to pay for purchases);

Charge backs for "routing violations," which are incorrect procedures, such as wrong department numbers or wrong order numbers, that occur during shipping;

Reimbursement for discounts given to retail employees who purchase the manufacturer's products;

A contribution to workroom costs, which include the time required to display the manufacturer's products;

Manufacturer coverage of the shortages that result from theft, book inventory error, and so on;

Exchanging "slow sellers" for better styles;

Discounts on all purchases for "new stores."

Manufacturer's Role

The bargaining power of both the vendor and the retailer depends on a mutual need for each another. If a retailer feels it can replace a manufacturer's product, thereby protecting a certain amount of its sales objectives, that retailer deals from strength and can be extremely demanding.

The manufacturer must weigh all options, including the possible loss of a retail operation from its account list. The brand name manufacturers, whose products are very popular, will obviously be better able to deal from strength and deny any retailer requests that seem excessive.

Manufacturer's Bargaining Chips

The manufacturer brings certain strengths to the bargaining table, including the "good will" of its brand name. As such, a national advertisement from a manufacturer can represent free advertising for the retailer of the product. The benefits from these advertisements can result in increased profits for the retailer. A second, but related, bargaining chip is the possibility that the manufacturer may become "hot," as its products sell at a rapid pace. Once again, the retailer benefits from such developments.

CREATING A PARTNERSHIP: NEGOTIATING THE CONTRACT

Practical Considerations

The retailer may request that the manufacturer's gross margin equal or exceed the planned gross margin for the department. This is because the retailer's actual profits may not always reach the planned gross margin required to produce a profit. The manufacturer who agrees to a gross margin percentage based on planned, rather than actual, profit will find itself facing serious losses.

For instance, a retailer plans a gross margin of 40 percent. As a result of an unavoidable problem (e.g., a snowstorm) that closes stores for several days, the retailer sustains huge losses and has an actual gross margin of only 25 percent, which is a disastrous performance. If the manufacturer agreed to a gross margin of 40 percent of planned sales, the company will have to pay thousands of dollars to make up the difference between the planned and the actual gross margin.

Clearly, an agreement that provides for exceeding the store's *actual* gross margin percent is a more desirable arrangement. This way, if any severe circumstances arise, the manufacturer is in a better situation, as performance will be compared to the gross margin achieved during the period of adversity.

Thus, during a "gross margin" agreement meeting, the retailer may announce that the manufacturer is expected to meet the store's planned gross margin of 42 percent for the spring. A wise vendor would reply that it cannot be expected to guarantee a percentage that is not based on actual sales and must try to persuade the retailer to accept a "level gross margin performance." This means that no specific gross margin percentage is mentioned. Rather, the manufacturer guarantees a prearranged percent or point goal that is compared to the retailer's actual gross margin at the conclusion of the selling season. This puts both vendor and retailer on a level playing field.

If adverse conditions prevail and the retailer has a disappointing season, the manufacturer's guarantee is now compared to actual results. For example, a manufacturer guarantees that its gross margin will exceed the retailer's actual gross margin by two points. Thus, if the retailer has a poor selling season, the manufacturer only has to pay two points above the actual gross margin earned.

Readers should refer to the subsection, Calculating Gross Margin, in Chapter 3, Vendor Analysis: Measuring Profitability, to learn how specific dollars are calculated for this agreement.

Contracts

Vendor and manufacturer profitability contracts are very informal. They are seldom prepared by attorneys and are rarely even signed documents. The astute retailer should request written verification of any deal constructed with a supplier to have proof of a disputable "verbal deal." Also, if the parties that constructed a deal are no longer employees at a subsequent time, a written contract will still be active. Manufacturers are usually very hesitant to sign written contracts.

A sample contract, or agreement, for actual gross margin (often called **maintained markup (MMU),** or just margin) might be as follows:

> [Name of retailer] has entered into an agreement with [name of manufacturer]. The said manufacturer states that at the conclusion of the season, the actual gross margin will be at least 40 percent.

Sell . . . and Repent

The word "deal" implies concessions from both parties. Thus, after the retailer has itemized the required guarantees, the next move belongs to the vendor. Some manufacturers may find the retailer's requests for guaranteed profitability problematic. How does one predict the possible ramifications that affect retail sales? What is the potential downside for a manufacturer who guarantees the retailer's requests? How many thousands of dollars are at risk if the product does not reach specified sales goals? The manufacturer must answer these questions before concluding the deal.

An axiom in the world of buying and selling is "Sell . . . and Repent!" Simply put, it means that a manufacturer will try to sell as much product as possible to a retailer and worry about the consequences later. However, ducking one's head in the sand does not make problems disappear. A manufacturer must weigh the retailer's requests, and modify them when possible, to balance both the rewards (purchases) and consequences (when markdowns erode gross margin to an unprofitable level).

One option is for the manufacturer to mark up the selling price to the retailer and then offer the retailer reimbursements based on sales. The obvious problem is that no retailer wants to pay more than necessary for purchases. A more serious concern is that retailers will sever relationships with manufacturers who are guilty of charging different prices to different retailers for the same product.

Clearly, a manufacturer and retailer should agree to a "deal" based on its mutual profitability. If the retailer does require reimbursements at the conclusion of a season, how does it affect the manufacturer's profits in selling to this retailer? Many manufacturers use a predetermined percentage of total sales as a basic measure of its reimbursements. For example, a manufacturer calculates a refund policy of 3 percent of net sales. Thus, if the manufacturer had shipments totaling $150,000 for a certain season, then 3 percent of that amount can be refunded (in the form of a markdown dollar allowance) to that retailer, as shown below:

$$\$150,000 \times 3\% = \$4,500 \text{ available}$$

INSIDE SCOOP

The Buyer-Vendor Relationship

Ira Lindner presents the retailer's point of view in terms of perceived violations of the purchase order contract. Todd Bernstein puts these violations into the context of issues that can affect the profitability of the retailer and the manufacturer.

Ira Lindner

Ira Lindner, a former owner of a men's retail store chain, is currently senior account executive at a major apparel manufacturer.

A significant source of friction between retail buyers and manufacturers is the buyer's claim that the manufacturer failed to adhere to the terms of the purchase order contract. The retailer now has merchandise it cannot sell; the manufacturer tries to avoid taking merchandise back. Among the retailer's complaints are the following:

1. The manufacturer does not ship the proper style, color, or sizes of the merchandise ordered. This is a violation of the purchase order, and retailers will demand to return the shipment. Manufacturers, however, are loathe to accept returns, particularly if they have borrowed against these shipments (called "factoring your receivables") and would therefore have to reimburse the factor for any returns.

2. The manufacturer fails to ship any merchandise at all, particularly when the product is imported. The

retailer now has a severe problem, as the department will be under stocked—and under-stocking makes it impossible for the buyer to reach his or her sales goals.

3. The manufacturer ships the order late. This puts the manufacturer in peril, as the retailer has the right to reject the shipment. Often, the retailer will request a discount before accepting the product.

4. The manufacturer does not ship the product as shown. Often, a manufacturer will show a "perfect" sample, but the actual product has "quality" problems. If a retailer contends that there are quality problems, it may take expensive litigation to settle the issue.

5. The manufacturer did not follow shipping instructions. This is a common, but much less serious, issue. These infractions include not labeling the shipping cartons with all of the information requested by the retailer.

6. The manufacturer's product does not sell to the consumer.

Todd Bernstein
Todd Bernstein is a senior account executive for Hugo Boss.

As evidenced in the preceding point of view, the relationship between the buyer (retailer) and the seller (vendor) is crucial to the success of every product. Vendors must understand and address the needs of the retailer. The retailer, on the other hand, must remember that the products being sold are the sole purpose of the retailer's existence. No products result in no stores; wrong products result in no business.

Five main points mold the relationship between vendors and buyers: return policies, charge back policies, terms of payments, markdown allowances, and guaranteed gross margin agreements. These determine how a buyer and seller interact on a daily basis. Relationships are everything, and both sides ultimately have the same goal: to make as much money as possible.

Return policies specifically for damaged goods and slow-selling products are common. It usually goes without saying that quality issues are dealt with on a case-by-case basis. In most cases neither the retailer nor the vendor wants something of inferior quality presented to the public. If the quality is questionable, a discount might be negotiated. As for slow sellers, both sides are responsible for deciding which products reach the public; therefore it is the fault of both if something does not sell well. Does the retailer take the hit? Does the vendor take the hit? This depends on the severity of "just how bad is it?" In most cases the vendor will swap the product for other merchandise. This is the best solution for both parties. The retailer receives more products to sell, and the vendor simply moves around some inventory.

Charge backs for vendor mistakes, such as purchase order violations (i.e., late delivery, mishandling, or misshipping) is a huge issue that constantly comes up for discussion. When a retailer charges a vendor back, the retailer is refusing to pay a certain amount of money based on a violation of rules that the retailer has set up. Legitimate charge backs are approved when product is late or the vendor makes a legitimate mistake. In many cases, distribution charge backs are negotiated the same way a delivery service negotiates its parking tickets.

Terms of payments can be looked at in two ways. The first is the length of time a retailer has before paying invoices. Usually, terms are decided at the time an order is placed. Net 30 or Net 60 means that a retailer has 30 days or 60 days respectively to pay an invoice. Very often a vendor will offer an incentive to a retailer, such as a discount, to pay sooner than the stated terms. The second way to understand terms of payment is to determine by what means a vendor is planning to handle shortage (theft) and employee discounts. Often, a vendor agrees to pay or split the shortage, as well as employee discounts, with the retailer. These agreements directly affect the gross margin, and, depending on what both sides decide, will make a difference when discussing markdown allowances and guaranteed gross margins.

Markdown allowances and guaranteed gross margin are intertwined. When retailers decide to do business with a vendor, they often want protection from sales falling short of expectations. Thus, in the event that the product fails, the vendor is expected to cover the retailer's cost to liquidate the merchandise. This is called a **markdown allowance**. On the flip side, when a vendor wants to do business with a specific retailer, the vendor will often offer a guaranteed gross margin, which protects the retailer from failure. The problems come when a retailer wants protection and the vendor refuses to provide it. This is almost always negotiated before a retailer places an order. Some retailers only want to buy what they want despite a guaranteed gross margin. Some vendors only want to sell to stores that have the potential to sell their products successfully.

Ultimately all these issues require heavy negotiating. The relationship between the buyer (retailer) and the seller (vendor) becomes increasingly important to a growing business. Both sides depend on each other to make money. Neither wins if both lose.

EXERCISES

1. Explain the difference between a gross margin guarantee that is based upon the planned margin and one based on actual gross margin.

2. Explain why a manufacturer should only guarantee a specific **markdown percentage** after the retailer has mentioned its goal.

3. A handbag manufacturer has a new retail account that is late in making its first payment for goods purchased. What should the manufacturer do?

4. A large retail chain has offered to buy large quantities of a new spring sportswear line. The buyer only purchases from vendors that guarantee a gross margin deal with their product. Prepare a list of questions that the buyer must answer before the manufacturer can reach a decision.

5. Why is gross margin so important?

6. Suppose a key retail account approaches a manufacturer after a particularly "poor season," states that the manufacturer's gross margin was extremely poor, and requests a huge reimbursement of money. If no deal existed between the retailer and manufacturer, how prudent would it be for the manufacturer to say "We had no deal in force. Therefore I will not consider compensating you"?

7. In researching a demand for monetary reimbursement to a retailer, the sales executive of a manufacturer discovered that the manufacturer had shipments totaling $220,000 to the retailer. If a 5 percent rebate of sales was agreed to, how much did the retailer receive?

8. A manufacturer calculated a 41 percent gross margin on its retail account. However, the retailer claimed there was a 37 percent gross margin. The manufacturer knew its sales and cost of sales numbers were accurate. What could explain the discrepancy?

9. Should a manufacturer send the retailer a check for markdowns?

10. In a plan to increase its gross margin, a manufacturer tells a retailer to increase its initial markup. Explain how this suggestion could backfire for the manufacturer.

11. A retailer in a ski resort asks for a set gross margin percentage before any purchases are made. As a manufacturer, what, if any, reservations might you have about agreeing to this request?

12. A new vendor shows a buyer the most wonderful merchandise at the cheapest possible cost. If successful, this merchandise could turn the entire season around. The buyer suggests placing the retailer's entire **open to buy (OTB)** on this merchandise. Is the buyer's suggestion correct, or can you foresee a potential disaster for the retailer?

PROJECTS

1. A major retail chain wishes to place a large order for a product. The buyer makes the following requests:

   a. The vendor will guarantee a gross margin of 45 percent.

   b. The vendor's payment will be held until the retailer is satisfied that the vendor's product adheres to gross margin guarantee.

   QUESTION: Assume you are the vendor. If you were asked to accept the terms specified above, explain your response and any modifications you might propose.

   NOTE: This problem requires careful examination and evaluation of the offer in order to plan your response. This project can only be satisfied when a wide range of options are examined.

2. The class will be divided into two groups. One group acts as a major retailer; the other as a swimsuit manufacturer. The retailer is considering a large investment (purchase) with the manufacturer. Assignments:

   a. The group representing the retailer should present the manufacturer with a list of the guarantees it requires before the purchase can be made.

   b. The group representing the manufacturer should try to restructure the deal so that it is less risky.

   c. Each group should negotiate a deal satisfactory to both parties.

The profitability of an item or group of items can only be determined after it is sold, because gross margin dollars can only be evaluated after both sales and markdowns have been calculated. As is clear from any **profit-and-loss (P/L) statement,** gross margin dollars must cover all operating expenses and still yield a profit. The retailer will also examine expected vendor margins and compare the vendor's performance with the retailer's goals. Remember that any analysis must account for every piece of merchandise that has been sold or marked down. Inventory not yet sold cannot be included in these analyses. The exception is at the conclusion of the season, when many unsold items are projected as sales and markdowns to clear aged merchandise.

MAINTAINED MARKUP/GROSS MARGIN

Many retailers and vendors use these terms interchangeably, but the terms have slightly different meanings.

Calculating Maintained Markup

Maintained markup (MMU) is calculated using markdown (MD) percentage and **initial markup percentage (IMU)** as follows:

$$MMU\% = IMU\% - (MD\% \times \text{complement of } IMU\%)$$

This formula yields a false "true cost," because the IMU percentage is not always adjusted to include the retailer's discount nor does it include certain retailer deductions, such as shortages and workroom costs, or markdown dollars given by the vendor.

Calculating Gross Margin

In contrast, gross margin is calculated as follows:

$$GM = \text{Net sales} - \textbf{Total cost of goods sold}$$

INSIDE SCOOP

Poor Gross Margins

Much of this text is concerned with achieving a gross margin that has produced enough dollars to allow for a profit. However, the reasons for a poor gross margin, from both the retailer's and the manufacturer's perspective, should also be discussed.

The manufacturer may deliver a product that is faulty. The problem can range from a hammer that breaks upon impact when striking a nail to a pair of pants with three legs. A common mistake is producing clothing that does not fit properly. Every new garment is supposed to have been submitted to a "fit model" for verification of the product's design. Further, before any actual production begins, a production prototype from the actual factory producing the order must be approved by a technician. Often, a manufacturer will have "freelance" technicians on call, as opposed to having full-time staff, to perform this service.

Much of the clothing sold to U.S. residents has been man-

ufactured in another country. Often the production of the product is separated by an ocean from the design elements. This leaves much room for error. To ensure quality, input from competent individuals at every phase of design and production is required.

Another complaint arises if the manufacturer ships an order "late" (that is, past the completion date specified on the buyer's order). As a result, product could arrive when it is no longer desired and will not sell. For example, a retailer in Seattle has little use for swimsuits shipped in September.

The retailer also has concerns. They include the unpredictability of weather, the general state of the economy, and poor judgment by buyers. Poor weather can inflict damage by keeping the consumer out of the store until the product loses its appeal and consumers now want something new.

To establish and maintain a good relationship between retailer and manufacturer requires an understanding of these issues, quality control throughout the production process, good communications, and a professional and amicable means of resolving issues.

Thus, the gross margin percentage, which includes deductions and is adjusted for markdowns, is often more accurate in determining true cost. The gross margin can also be affected by the retailer's inclusion of costs that manufacturers argue should not be standard in gross margin analysis. Such costs may include employee discounts, shortages in inventory after either a book or **physical inventory,** and workroom costs. The latter are costs associated with preparing items for display, such as steaming silk dresses. Thus, before conducting any analysis of vendor or profitability performance, the manufacturer must be cognizant of the retailer's gross margin formulation.

COMPUTATION OF EXPECTED SALES

To analyze a vendor's success, the retailer must be able to convert purchases into the correct dollar amount of sales necessary to reach the gross margin plan. Every retail purchase by a buyer has an implicit expectation of sales. In this context, sales includes the full price sales, as well as sales at various markdown rates. Each purchase is, in effect, a microcosm of the entire store's income statement and must produce the planned gross margin.

The only tools needed to determine expected sales are knowledge of a retailer's purchases and the planned markdown percentage. The retail purchase is divided by the number "1" plus the actual markdown percentage expressed as a decimal. In some cases, only the retailer's maintained markup percentage and initial markup percentage are known. In these cases, the missing markdown percentage should be calculated using the maintained markup formula.

Example

A retailer places an order totaling $100,000 at retail with a vendor. This retailer has a departmental markdown of 32 percent. To compute expected sales, divide retail purchases by 1.32 in this case. The results yield both the sales and markdown dollars on the $100,000 purchase. Remember that only one correct sales amount can fulfill the mathematical requirements of this equation correctly.

$$\frac{\text{Retail purchase}}{1 + \text{MD\%}} \quad \frac{\$100,000}{1.32} = \$75,758$$

Thus, this retailer's purchase should result in sales of $75,758. This purchase can now be analyzed as follows:

Retail purchases = $100,000

Departmental markdown = 32%

Total sales = $75,758

To find the markdown dollars, subtract the sales dollars from total retail purchases:

$100,000 − $75,758 = $24,242

To check your calculations, divide the markdown dollars by sales. This will give you the markdown percentage.

$$\frac{\$24,242}{\$75,758} = 32\%$$

The five practice problems that follow focus first on computing the markdown and then on computing expected sales. Solutions are provided for the first three; you should complete the last two questions on your own.

Problem #1

A retailer has an initial markup of 52 percent and is planning a maintained markup of 40 percent. Find the markdown percentage.

Solution

Use the maintained markup formula to find the markdown percentage.

$$MMU\% = IMU\% - (X \times \text{complement of IMU\%})$$
$$.40 = .52 - (X \times .48)$$
$$.40 = .52 - .48X$$
$$.48X = .52 - .40$$
$$.48X = .12$$
$$X = .25 = 25\%$$

Now that the markdown percentage is known, sales expectations can be calculated. The following problem provides practice in breaking down retail purchases into sales and markdown components.

Problem #2

A New York handbag manufacturer took an order from a retailer totaling $160,000 at retail, with a guaranteed gross margin of 42 percent and an initial markup of 51 percent. Even before the season began, the manufacturer was able to calculate the dollar expectations for future reference by determining the markdown percentage and the markdown in dollars. Can you make these same calculations?

Solution

STEP 1 Find the markdown percentage using the maintained markup formula:

$$.42 = .51 - (X \times .49)$$
$$.42 = .51 - .49X$$
$$.49X = .51 - .42$$
$$.49X = .09$$
$$X = 0.1837 = 18.37\%$$

STEP 2 Use the calculated markdown percentage to convert "retail purchases" into "retail sales." This is accomplished by dividing retail purchases by "1" added to the actual markdown percentage expressed as a decimal.

$$\frac{\$160,000}{1.1837} = \$135,169 \text{ Retail sales}$$

STEP 3 Find the markdown dollars by subtracting retail sales from retail purchases.

$160,000	Retail purchases
− $135,169	Retail sales
$ 24,831	Markdown

STEP 4 Find the gross margin dollars by subtracting sales minus cost:

Cost = $160,000 × .49 (complement of IMU)
Cost = $ 78,400

Sales	$135,169
− Cost	$ 78,400
GM	$ 56,769

Problem #3

Find the sales amount and markdown dollars if retail purchases equal $80,000 and the markdown plan is 28 percent. First compute the sales, then the markdown dollars, and finally double-check your answer.

Solution

$$\frac{\$80,000}{1.28} = \$62,500 \text{ Sales}$$

$$\$80,000 - \$62,500 = \$17,500 \text{ MD}$$

$$\frac{\$17,500}{\$62,500} = 28\%$$

Problem #4

Find total sales and markdown dollars if retail purchases total $260,000 and the departmental markdown rate is 29.5 percent.

Solution

PLANNED VERSUS ACTUAL GOALS

Never forget that a retailer's planned gross margin is often not achieved. However, as a negotiating tool, the shrewd retailer will request monetary compensation as part of a contract based on planned, rather than actual, goals.

If a retailer has a plan to reach a departmental gross margin percentage goal of 40 percent, the retailer will often use this "planned" percentage in determining manufacturer profitability, even though the actual gross margin was less. This is extremely advantageous to the retailer, as it demands an unrealistic performance level from its suppliers.

Problem #5

Find total sales and markdown dollars if retail purchases total $140,000 and **planned markdown (PMD)** is 31.5 percent.

Solution

PROFITABILITY

Most vendor analysis and profitability reports are presented in one of three ways:

1. The retailer combines all of the months in a particular season and recaps the various categories under examination.
2. The retailer's performance with a manufacturer is presented in a monthly flow chart.
3. The Retailer's Report Card is used; this is a profitability analysis that compares all the vendors in a particular department according to several categories of performance.

The student of retail mathematics, the retail buyer, and the manufacturer's sales representative must understand all of the procedures. The seasonal and monthly approaches are explained in the following scenarios. See Chapter 4 for a discussion of the Retailer's Report Card.

The Seasonal Analysis

A vendor's profitability is most commonly analyzed seasonally. As such, months with a lower profitability are averaged with months of higher profitability so that the cumulative result more accurately reflects the total picture.

Before a purchase order is written, the retailer meets with the manufacturer to create performance guidelines. Most often, the retailer sets goals in the form of expected gross margin.

For example, a large department store chain, headquartered in New York, was considering a sizeable purchase of a very popular brand name junior dress from "Howe's Line," if the manufacturer guaranteed an actual gross margin of 38 percent. The manufacturer readily agreed. This retailer worked on an initial markup of 53 percent and had markdowns of 31.9 percent. The retailer made retail purchases totaling $140,000. As the manufacturer began to ship the product, all sales and markdowns were scrupulously maintained. As the season progressed, the competent sales representative asked the buyer for statistical reports (selling records). Because the buyer had a **turn** goal, sales were evaluated weekly. After a month, enough information was available to make assumptions about whether seasonal goals could be met.

At the conclusion of the selling season, the retailer prepares a profitability report for each vendor. The retailer's vendor analysis for Howe's Line was as follows:

Retail purchases = $140,000

IMU = 53%

Planned GM = 38%

Actual GM = 37%

MD needed = $1,660

This analysis indicates that the manufacturer missed the guaranteed gross margin by 1 percent. Therefore, this gross margin needs an allowance of $1,660 to conform to the agreed-upon profitability.

Is the markdown allowance of $1,660 a legitimate request? To answer that question, actual gross margin dollars must be compared with planned gross margin dollars. Thus, it is necessary to determine what the sales amount would be at both actual (37 percent) and planned (38 percent) gross margin percentages. To do this, the total cost of the purchases must first be calculated:

Cost = $140,000 × .47 = $65,800 (53% complement of IMU)

Using the maintained markup formula, calculate the actual and planned markdown percentage at the given IMU and MMU:

When Gross Margin = 37%	When Gross Margin = 38%
$.37 = .53 - (X \times .47)$	$.38 = .53 - (X \times .47)$
$.37 = .53 - .47X$	$.38 = .53 - .47X$
$.47X = .53 - .37$	$.47X = .53 - .38$
$.47X = .16$	$.47X = .15$
$X = 34\%$	$X = 31.9\%$

Gross margin dollars, at both planned and actual goals, can be calculated by using the markdown percentages to determine the sales expected at each percentage and then subtracting the cost.

Thus,

$$\frac{\$140,000}{1.319} = \quad \$106,141 \text{ (38\% GM)}$$
$$- \quad 65,800 \text{ (Cost)}$$
$$\$ \ 40,341 \text{ (Planned GM\$)}$$

$$\frac{\$140,000}{1.34} = \quad \$104,478 \text{ (Sales at 37\% GM)}$$
$$- \quad 65,800 \text{ (Cost)}$$
$$\$ \ 38,678 \text{ (Actual GM\$)}$$

The chart can now be completed as follows:

Planned GM$	Actual GM$	Dollar Difference
$40,341	$38,678	$1,663

Thus, the retailer's calculation of the deficiency is accurate, and the retailer would probably issue a markdown allowance request in that amount. The manufacturer usually makes some attempt to lower the dollar request or to offer some other kind of allowance, such as a discount on future prices, but most often the retailer will demand the markdown dollars.

Problem #6

A California-based popularly priced men's shirt manufacturer received the following profitability report from a major retail chain. The retailer claimed that the actual selling and planned markdown goals were not achieved. Note the following:

Retailer's goals:
IMU   = 55.5%
PMD   = 28.0%
Actual sales = $105,000
Actual MD = $31,500

1. Based on this information:

   a. Does the manufacturer owe the retailer any money?

   b. If yes, how much money is owed?

2. Find the GM.

Solution

1. This a very straightforward problem.

   a. The actual markdown percentage is markdown dollars ÷ sales:

   $$\frac{\$\ 31,500}{\$105,000} = 30\%$$

   Thus, the actual markdown was 2 percent greater than planned.

   b. To calculate the correct amount of planned sales dollars, find the total retail purchases (sales plus markdowns) and divide by 1.28. Thus,

   $$\$105,000 + \$31,500 = \frac{\$136,500}{1.28} = \$106,641$$

   If a markdown of 28 percent had been achieved, the correct amount of sales would have been $106,641. To find how much the manufacturer owes the retailer, subtract actual sales from planned sales:

Planned sales	$106,641
− Actual sales	$105,000
Difference	$ 1,641

   NOTE: You did not have to compare the markdown dollars specifically because the difference between actual and planned sales will always equal the difference between the actual and planned markdowns.

2. The following two methods can be used to determine gross margin:

Method #1	Method #2
GM = Sales − Cost	
$105,000	$X = .555 - (.30 \times .445)$
− 60,743	$X = .555 - .1335$
$ 44,257 GM	$X = .4215$
GM% = 42.15	GM% = 42.15

NOTE: Cost is calculated by finding total retail purchases, in this case 136,500, adding sales plus markdowns, and finally using the complement of IMU to find the cost of 60,743.

REMEMBER: Sales + MDs = Retail purchases

The Monthly Flow Chart

This type of profitability analysis presents a unique problem for the manufacturer. Unlike the seasonal analysis, which averages the profits of several months, this scenario requires that each month must stand on its own. Compare the two methods for a buyer who receives his or her spring merchandise in January, but has a poor sales month because of severe snow storms. In the "seasonal analysis" method, the poor performance in January will be averaged with higher profits in later months; the season, as a whole, will prove profitable. However, in a monthly flow evaluation, each month is evaluated separately. Thus, a retailer could request monetary compensation at the end of January.

Problem #7

A large specialty store chain in Texas made a deal with a Chicago-based manufacturer that included a guaranteed gross margin of 40 percent. As previously discussed, establishing a "fixed" gross margin percentage gives an immediate advantage to the retailer even before the retailer places the order. The advantage to the retailer is that the manufacturer is held to the guarantee whether or not the selling season is successful. The manufacturer has no safety belt that allows for

MARKDOWN MONEY

It is ironic that although profit is measured by gross margins (also called vendor margins), the remunerations are commonly called "markdown money." Markdowns, when controlled, are a normal part of business. A store or department changes from season to season through sales and markdowns. No matter how successful a buyer was in making purchases, a certain amount of product must always be drastically reduced or, in fact, given away.

Markdowns are controlled by carefully calculating the proper initial markup by using the following formula:

$$IMU = \frac{GM\ plan + MD\ plan}{Net\ sales + MD\ plan}$$

For example, last season Joe's Jeans had markdowns of 30 percent. If the store's goal is a gross margin of 40 percent, the formula is set up as follows:

$$IMU = \frac{.4 + .3}{1 + .3} = \frac{.7}{1.3} = 53.8\%$$

The IMU should be 53.8 percent, as this will yield the proper gross margin of 40 percent after the planned markdowns erode the IMU.

a sliding-scale adjustment to the promised gross margin percentage in a poor retail season. Remember that BOM means the beginning of month, and TMH means the total merchandise handled.

Note the following May projection:

$$
\begin{aligned}
\text{BOM} &= \$120,000 \\
+\ \text{New receipts} &= \$\ \ 62,000 \\
\hline
\text{TMH} &= \$182,000 \\
-\ \text{Sales} &= \$\ \ 58,000 \\
-\ \text{MDS} &= \$\ \ 22,000 \\
\hline
\text{EOM} &= \$102,000
\end{aligned}
$$

The above retailer works on a 53 percent IMU. As the manufacturer, your agreement is to equal or exceed a gross margin of 40 percent. The retailer tells you that the calculations above require $3,000 at cost to reach the store's gross margin goals. Should you grant it?

Solution
Calculate gross margin percentage

STEP 1 Ascertain the cost of the merchandise sold. To obtain that figure, add sales and markdowns. Thus, $58,000 + $22,000 = $80,000. This represents the total amount of merchandise involved in this analysis. Because the initial markup is given as 53 percent, the cost of the merchandise sold can be calculated using the cost calculation formula:

Retail $\times$ complement of initial markup = cost
$80,000 $\times$ .47 = $37,600

STEP 2 Now that the cost of the merchandise sold has been calculated at $37,600, that number can be used to calculate the actual gross margin percentage by using the basic gross margin formula:

Net sales $-$ Cost of merchandise sold = GM$
$58,000 $-$ $37,600 = $20,400 GM$

STEP 3 Now, calculate the gross margin actual percentage, using the familiar formula:

$$\frac{\text{GM\$}}{\text{Net sales}} = \text{Gross margin percentage}$$

$$\frac{\$20,400}{\$58,000} = 35.17\%$$

ANALYSIS Your actual achieved gross margin percentage is less than the 40 percent margin to which you agreed.

Check the veracity of the retailer's request for $3,000 in markdown money.

STEP 1 Check the retailer's request of $3,000 at cost against the actual sales and determine if the resulting gross margin is in line with the agreement. Therefore, calculate:

Actual sales + MD$ request = Sales stated in agreement
$58,000 + $3,000 = $61,000

STEP 2 Use this figure to recalculate the adjusted gross margin percentage:

$$
\begin{array}{r}
\$61,000 \\
-\ \ 37,600 \\
\hline
\$23,400
\end{array}
\qquad
\frac{\$23,400}{61,000} = 38.36\%
$$

Now, restate the information as follows:

Planned Gross Margin	Actual Gross Margin	"Adjusted" Gross Margin
40%	35.17%	38.36%

QUESTION: Should the retailer receive its markdown request of $3,000?

ANSWER: Yes, because even with the $3,000 markdown adjustment, the manufacturer is still below the agreed on gross margin of 40 percent. In fact, the retailer could ask for additional funds so that the 40 percent margin would be reached.

Problem #8

A major retailer in Florida has entered into a partnership with a jewelry manufacturer for the fall season. The manufacturer has agreed to conform to the retailer's request not to exceed a markdown of 25 percent. The retailer works on a 52 percent IMU. This problem represents a type of biased method practiced by some retailers; it is discussed in greater detail in Chapter 4. Turn equals sales divided by average monthly inventory. For more information on the concept of turn, see Chapter 6.

Review the following flow chart and then answer the following:

1. Calculate each month's MD%, MMU%, and turn.
2. Calculate the season's MD%, MMU%, and turn.
3. In September, the retailer explains that the manufacturer has a markdown percentage rate of 38 percent and asks for $5,000 at cost to offset markdowns. What should the manufacturer do?

	July	August	September
BOM	74,000	82,000	82,000
+ New receipts	52,000	39,000	41,000
TMH	126,000	121,000	123,000
− Sales	40,000	33,000	29,000
− MD	4,000	6,000	11,000
EOM	82,000	82,000	83,000
MD%			
MMU%			
Turn			

Solution

1. Perform the monthly calculations as follows:
   a. For MD%, divide markdown dollars by sales.

b. For MMU%, add sales and markdowns. Then multiply the result by the IMU **complement** to find the cost. Then, subtract cost from sales and divide the difference by sales.

c. For turn, divide sales by average monthly inventory. (Find the average monthly inventory by adding BOM to EOM and dividing by two.)

$$\frac{BOM + EOM}{2} = \text{Average monthly inventory}$$

$$\text{Turn} = \frac{Sales}{\text{Average monthly inventory}}$$

The completed flow chart looks as follows:

	July	August	September
BOM	74,000	82,000	82,000
+ New receipts	52,000	39,000	41,000
TMH	126,000	121,000	123,000
− Sales	40,000	33,000	29,000
− MD	4,000	6,000	11,000
EOM	82,000	82,000	83,000
MD%	10.00%	18.18%	37.93%
MMU%	47.20%	43.27%	33.79%
Turn	.51	.40	.35

2. Perform the season calculations as follows.

a. Divide the total MD dollars for the three months by the total sales for the three months:

$$MD\% = \frac{\$\,21,000}{\$102,000} = 20.6\%$$

b. To find the cost of the total sales, add sales plus markdowns and multiply by the cost complement:

$$\$123,000 \times .48 = \$59,040 \text{ cost}$$

$$\frac{\text{Sales} - \text{Cost}}{\text{Sales}} = \text{MMU\%}$$

$$\$102,000 - \$59,040 = \frac{42,960}{102,000} = 42.1\%$$

Therefore,

   c. To calculate turn for a three-month period, add the BOM of each month to the EOM of September, then divide by four.

$$\text{Turn} = \frac{\text{Sales}}{\text{Average inventory}} = \frac{\$102,000}{\$80,250} = 1.27$$

3. The retailer is correct that the manufacturer far exceeded the markdown percentage agreement in September. Thus, the manufacturer might, at first, grant the retailer's request. If, however, all three months are reviewed together, the combined markdown percentage would be as follows:

$$\frac{\text{Total MD for three months}}{\text{Total sales for three months}} \quad \frac{\$\ 21,000}{\$102,000} = 20.6\%$$

REASON VERSUS STATISTICS

Sometimes a manufacturer may have respectable profits, but still be experiencing a significant drop in the volume of sales. Why? Because purchasing can be subjective. Past records may not be accurate indicators of future purchases, as buyers may decide that the current merchandise does not have the appeal of the previous product.

The buyer who makes such a decision and thereby chooses to ignore a previously profitable vendor should be sure about his or her actions, because once the buyer commits to a purchasing plan, there will be immediate backlash from the manufacturer. The manufacturer, who will suffer from the loss of business, is going to expect an explanation and may well go over the head of the buyer for an answer.

This second approach shows that the three-month period was profitable; the markdown was only 20.6 percent. Thus, manufacturers should always ask to have profitability reviewed on a seasonal basis. A manufacturer who is evaluated monthly is in a no-win situation. Although the manufacturer may have some very profitable months, it will be difficult to use those months to offset less profitable periods.

This is made perfectly clear by an analysis of the problem just concluded. Taken as a season and averaged, the markdown percentage was 20.6. However, if one looks only at September, the markdowns ran 37.93 percent. Thus, no markdown money is required by the seasonal analysis, but if based on a monthly analysis, September would be "red flagged" and the retailer would request a markdown allowance.

EXERCISES

1. If your department had an IMU of 53 percent and planned mark-downs of 28 percent, find the maintained markup.

2. What maintained markup will be produced by an IMU of 49.5 percent and markdowns of 26 percent?

3. Find the markdown percentage if the IMU is 54.5 percent and the maintained markup is 42 percent.

4. Find the markdown percentage if the IMU is 52 percent and the maintained markup is 38 percent.

5. A retail purchase totaling $84,000 has a markdown plan of 30 percent. Find the projected sales and the expected markdown dollars.

6. A retailer makes a purchase at cost of $171,429. The IMU is 54.5 percent and markdowns are planned at 32 percent. Find the expected sales and markdown dollars.

7. A manufacturer and a retailer agree to a seasonal actual mark-down of 30 percent. At the conclusion of the season, the results were:

Retail purchases = $102,000

Plan MD = 30%

Actual MD = 33%

Find the dollar differential of the planned to actual markdown percentage.

8. A retailer and a manufacturer agreed on a 28 percent markdown. If retail purchases totaled $180,000 and the actual markdown was 34 percent, find the dollar differential between the planned and actual markdown.

9. A retailer and manufacturer agree on a gross margin of 42 percent. Based on the season's results below, find the dollar differential between the planned and actual gross margin.

    Retail purchases = $200,000
    IMU = 52%
    Planned GM = 42%
    Actual GM = 38%

10. A retailer presented the following seasonal profitability report to a vendor. Based on these numbers, find the dollar difference between the planned and actual gross margin percentages.

    Retail purchases = $310,000
    IMU = 54.5%
    Guaranteed GM% = 44%
    Actual GM% = 41%

A retailer presented a vendor with the following monthly flow chart.
Based on this information, answer questions 11 through 14.

	May	IMU = 52%
BOM	106,000	
+ New receipts	41,000	
TMH	147,000	
− Sales	44,000	
− MD	11,000	
EOM	92,000	

11. Find the markdown percentage.

12. Find the maintained markup percentage.

13. Find average inventory.

14. If the retailer stated that the month's markdowns ran too high and markdown dollars are requested, how might a clever manufacturer postpone the markdown request?

PROJECTS

1. Explain the statement: "Every dollar of markdown increases the cost of merchandise sold by the same amount."

2. Explain the statement: "The cost of sales must always include the cost of markdown."

CHAPTER 4 / Retailer's Report Card

As a result of computers, retailers can now access information on the profitability of each vendor and each department in a variety of configurations. Although most retailers have their own methods of evaluating a manufacturer's performance, every method assesses the following key factors:

1. The manufacturer's total retail sales
2. The gross margin percentage maintained
3. The penetration of the percentage of sales compared with the percentage of purchases

Manufacturers anxiously await these "profitability report cards" because future business is based on them. Manufacturers whose products earn a larger proportion of retail sales compared to a proportionate amount of stock will see an increase in retail purchases. The manufacturer should know how such reports are computed before signing a contract and should know how to verify the retailer's analysis of profitability.

After a retail purchase or purchases are put on the selling floor, all transactions are noted. Purchases are sold and marked down until the season ends and profitability is analyzed. Markdowns are carefully calculated whether permanent or by point of sale. The following is an example of how sales and markdowns may be tracked:

Retail purchases = $200,000

40% sold at full price

30% sold at 25% off

30% sold at 40% off

Percentage of Purchase		Sales	Markdowns
(40%)	$80,000 (full price)	$ 80,000	0
(30%)	$60,000 (25% off)	$ 45,000	$15,000
(30%)	$60,000 (40% off)	$ 36,000	$24,000
Totals		$161,000	$39,000

POINT OF SALE

A retailer usually takes markdowns, either permanently or for a short period of time. A permanent or "hard" markdown is physically recorded on the ticket price. If a retailer wishes to promote a selection of merchandise to stimulate sales, but does not wish the merchandise to remain at the markdown price, a "point of sale" markdown is put into effect.

Generally the retailer posts the limited time markdown using price cards. The language used may be "30% off today only" or "Mother's Day special 25% discount." With limited-time markdowns, the prices on the tickets attached to the individual items are not changed. When a sale item is brought to a cashier, the markdown is applied manually. Thus, the markdown occurs at the time of sale.

Whichever method is used, markdowns must be carefully noted. If they are not, the buyer's year-end physical inventory will be significantly different than that indicated on the book records.

Thus, the retail purchase has ended with sales of $161,000 and markdowns of $39,000. This information is computer-generated and the buyers are given this profitability analysis information. A synopsis may appear as follows:

$$\text{Retail purchases} = \$200,000$$
$$\text{Sales} = \$161,000$$
$$\text{MDs} = \$39,000$$
$$\text{IMU} = 52\%$$
$$\text{MMU} = 40.4\%$$

Note that the IMU is needed to supply the maintained markup summary. To negotiate future deals, a buyer or division merchandise manager for the retailer will present the report to the manufacturer's sales manager or account representative.

EVALUATING A RETAILER'S REPORT CARD

To evaluate a retailer's report card, the manufacturer should take the following steps.

STEP 1 Calculate the gross margin percentage for each vendor.

EXAMPLE:

GM% for vendor A:

	Sales	$115,000
−	Cost	$ 70,000
	GM$	$ 45,000
		$115,000 Sales

$$\text{GM} = 39.1\%$$

STEP 2 Find each vendor's rate in order of percentage of open to buy (inventory).

STEP 3 Find each vendor's placement by percentage of sales as determined by retailer's analysis of profitability.

Problem

You are the coat buyer for a major store. Last fall, you purchased from six vendors with the following results:

Vendor	Cost Spent	Retail Sales	GM	% of OTB	% of Sales
A	70,000	115,000			
B	220,000	300,000			
C	100,000	175,000			
D	160,000	300,000			
E	60,000	95,000			
F	250,000	400,000			
Total					

Using the information contained in the vendor's report card, answer the following:

1. What is the gross margin percentage for the entire department?
2. Create a chart that compares each vendor's penetration of open to buy and sales.
3. You are given $900,000 at cost for next season's purchases. Based on the performance record of the six vendors, what percentage of open to buy would be planned for each of these vendors? Explain your decision.

REMINDER: To find each vendor's percentage to total either of sales or open to buy, determine the total cost spent or total sales obtained by each vendor and divide by the department total. Thus Vendor A's percentage of total open to buy is calculated as follows:

$$\text{Vendor A total cost} \quad \frac{\$\,70{,}000}{\$860{,}000} = 0.081$$
Divided by total costs

Vendor A was 8.1 percent of open to buy.

Solution

The completed report card looks as follows:

Vendor	Cost Spent	Retail Sales	GM	% of OTB	% of Sales
A	70,000	115,000	39.1%	8.1%	8.3%
B	220,000	300,000	26.7%	25.6%	21.7%
C	100,000	175,000	42.9%	11.6%	12.6%
D	160,000	300,000	46.7%	18.6%	21.7%
E	60,000	95,000	36.8%	7.0%	6.9%
F	250,000	400,000	37.5%	29.1%	28.9%
Total	860,000	1,385,000	37.9%		

1. Total gross margin percentage = Total sales − Total costs
   Therefore,

$$\begin{array}{r} \$1,385,000 \\ -\quad 860,000 \\ \hline \$\;\;525,000 \end{array} \qquad \frac{\$525,000}{1,385,000} = 37.9\% \text{ Departmental GM\%}$$

2. Ranking in order of vendors:

Percentage of Open to Buy	Percentage of Sales	GM%
F	F	D
B	B	C
D	D	A
C	C	F
A	A	E
E	E	B

3. Performance evaluation and future sales **volume** adjustments are as follows:

VENDOR A: This vendor was slightly above the average GM percentage. Depending on the content of Vendor A's new line, the purchase should range between $60,000 and $100,000.

VENDOR B: This vendor was the least profitable. Although there was a large proportion of open to buy, no profits were produced and losses were significant. There is no statistical reason to make future purchases from Vendor B unless the retailer feels this was an explainable and excusable performance.

VENDOR C: This vendor had an excellent performance. Future purchases should range between $150,000 and $200,000.

VENDOR D: This vendor was the most profitable. Future purchases should range between $225,000 and $250,000.

VENDOR E: The vendor hovers right below the average gross margin. Future purchases should be $60,000.

VENDOR F: This vendor required the most complicated merchandising decision of the six vendors. Although its performance was at just about the average departmental GM percentage, it represents almost one-third of total sales. To lower its volume would mean a large percentage of unprotected sales. Thus, although the performance was only slightly better than average, the vendor still provided a profit on a major portion of the buyer's purchases and retained its sales volume. Therefore, future purchases should range between $225,000 and $250,000.

INCLUSION OF A DISCOUNT

Many retailers receive a discount on their purchases from manufacturers. This could be in the form of a "trade discount," or a discount for paying invoices earlier than they are due. These "discounts," when thrown into the profitability mix, create some interesting and

ENTER THE ABYSS

Most salespeople, selling at wholesale for a manufacturer, are at one time or another confronted by a retail buyer whose expertise in determining profitability is impressive. In the world of retailer and wholesaler, the balance is heavily tipped toward the retailer in terms of academic acumen in the study of retail mathematics. Most retail buyers are schooled, and become proficient in, this most necessary mathematical exploration. Manufacturers should use this chapter to help balance the scale of knowledge by learning how to evaluate retailer's contractual demands and analyses of profit.

The case study in this chapter presents a profitability report from an actual company. Note that when the report was presented to the author, the manufacturer had already paid the retailer for the gross margin deficit. But in reviewing the report card, the author discovered an error in the computations that has now been corrected. These kinds of errors could be discovered if manufacturers better understood how to review such profitability reports.

INSIDE SCOOP

Analyzing a Profitability Report

Below is an actual profitability report from a major department store chain. Confidentiality requires that the retailer's and manufacturer's names not be printed.

	February 2002 Actual	March 2002 Projected	April 2002 Projected	Projected Sales
Sales $	6.6	19.0	21.0	46.6
Markdown $	−7.8	22.0	11.0	25.2
Markdown %	118.2%	118.2%	52.4%	54.0%
Markup %	52.4%	52.4%	52.4%	52.4%
PURCHASES	46.2	31.0	35.6	112.80
Cost	22.0	14.8	16.8	53.7
Less 8%	1.8	1.2	1.1	4.3
Net Cost	20.2	13.6	13.6	49.4
Retail	46.2	31.0	36.0	112.6
Net MU%	56.2%	56.2%	56.2%	56.2%
Comp of Net MU%	43.8%	43.8%	43.8%	43.8%
CMD% = MD$ * CNMU	−3.4	9.6	4.8	11.0
S:S * Net MU%	3.7	10.7	11.8	26.2
$ GM	7.1	1.0	7.0	15.2
= Vendor Margin %	108.0%	5.5%	33.3%	32.5%
Actual Vendor GM $	7.1	1.0	7.0	15.2
Store's GM Goal %	43.0	43.0%	43.0%	43.0%
Store's GM Goal $	2.8	8.2	9.0	20.0
$ Needed at Cost from Vendor	−4.3	7.1	2.0	4.8

PERMS   OH   % off $
DEC/JAN   2.3   25%   0.6
PLEASE CALL TO FINALIZE MDA BY 3/25
THANK YOU FOR YOUR SUPPORT

Based on this profitability report, which declares a gross margin deficit of 10.5 percent, the retailer is requesting $4,800 from the manufacturer. If you were the manufacturer, how would you examine this report to confirm or dispute the retailer's request? It is imperative to remember that every retailer uses its own method of reporting profitability. Therefore, manufacturers must learn to extrapolate the pertinent statistics and use mathematical formulas to verify the retailer's findings. The manufacturer should examine these reports by following the steps now described.

STEP 1: The most common starting point is verification of the actual markdown percentage. To determine this, we have highlighted the last column, "Projected Sales" (or projected profitability) to date, in the following chart.

	February 2002 Actual	March 2002 Projected	April 2002 Projected	Projected Sales
Sales $	6.6	19.0	21.0	46.6
Markdown $	−7.8	22.0	11.0	25.2
Markdown %	118.2%	118.2%	52.4%	54.0%
Markup %	52.4%	52.4%	52.4%	52.4%
PURCHASES	46.2	31.0	35.6	112.80
Cost	22.0	14.8	16.8	53.7
Less 8%	1.8	1.2	1.1	4.3
Net Cost	20.2	13.6	13.6	49.4
Retail	46.2	31.0	36.0	112.6
Net MU%	56.2%	56.2%	56.2%	56.2%
Comp of Net MU%	43.8%	43.8%	43.8%	43.8%
CMD% = MD$ * CNMU	−3.4	9.6	4.8	11.0
S:S * Net MU%	3.7	10.7	11.8	26.2
$ GM	7.1	1.0	7.0	15.2
= Vendor Margin %	108.0%	5.5%	33.3%	32.5%
Actual Vendor GM $	7.1	1.0	7.0	15.2
Store's GM Goal %	43.0	43.0%	43.0%	43.0%
Store's GM Goal $	2.8	8.2	9.0	20.0
$ Needed at Cost from Vendor	−4.3	7.1	2.0	4.8

PERMS   OH   % off $
DEC/JAN   2.3   25%   0.6
PLEASE CALL TO FINALIZE MDA BY 3/25
THANK YOU FOR YOUR SUPPORT

By using the markdown percentage formula (markdown dollars / sales), we can calculate the markdown percentage. That is the retailer's projected—or planned—markdown percentage, which may or may not be the amount actually achieved. The projected sales column indicates the markdown dollar amount to be $25,200, and the sales dollar amount to be $46,600. If these numbers are plugged into the markdown percentage formula, the result is:

$$\frac{\$25,200}{\$46,600} = \text{Markdown of } 54\%$$

Clearly, this computation confirms the analysis in the profitability report. To compare the profitability report with the manufacturer's computations, one must first confirm that the sales and markdown dollar figures are correct. Just because a report can be confirmed based on its numbers is not enough; first, the numbers themselves must be verified. That is accomplished by reviewing and certifying the monthly computations. Thus, it is essential in a professional buyer/vendor relationship that the retailer give the manufacturer ready access to weekly—or at least monthly—sales performances information. A signed agreement between a retailer and a vendor implies access to all pertinent information by all participants. If a manufacturer does not carefully monitor its products' selling performance at least every month, then the manufacturer will have no way to confirm the data presented by the Retailer's Report Card.

STEP 2: The next step is to confirm the actual gross margin percentage.

REMINDER: This retailer received a discount. Therefore, the manufacturer must verify that the retailer has allowed for the discount in preparing the profitability report, as all discounts benefit a manufacturer's profitability by lowering the cost of merchandise sold. Remember, every dollar saved in the cost price is reflected as an extra gross margin dollar.

By adding the projected sales and the projected markdowns for the period in question, the manufacturer can determine the value of the merchandise at retail. Thus, in the example:

$$46.6 + 25.2 = 71.8 \text{ or } \$71,800$$

Next, the manufacturer must determine the cost of merchandise sold as follows:

$$\$71,800 \times \text{complement of IMU} = \text{Cost}$$
$$\$71,800 \times 47.6\% = \$34,177$$

Next, apply the discount to the cost:

$$\$34,177 - 8\% \text{ discount} = \text{True cost}$$
$$\$34,177 - \$2,734 = \$31,443$$

Thus, the true cost of sales is \$31,443. To compute gross margin dollars, use the formula:

	Sales	\$46,600
−	CMS	31,443
	GM	\$15,157

To compute the gross margin percentage, divide gross margin dollars by net sales as follows:

$$\frac{\$15,157}{\$46,600} = 32.5\%$$

If this is compared to the vendor margin percentage in the last column of the chart, the retailer's statistic is confirmed. We have now confirmed the accuracy of the key elements of this profitability report.

STEP 3: Finally, the manufacturer needs to confirm the accuracy of the retailer's request for \$4,800 in vendor compensation, at cost. This means that the retailer has taken the retail dollars of compensation and converted it to cost terms. That is very beneficial to the manufacturer, as the total amount due to be paid by the manufacturer is based on the cost complement of the retail dollars requested. Many retailers charge the entire request at retail rather than at cost.

important dynamics. For example, suppose a retailer places an order for \$100,000 at cost. The manufacturer gives the retailer an 8 percent discount. In reality, if all product is shipped, the retailer would pay cost less the discount, or $\$100,000 \times .08 = \$8,000$. Because purchases at cost minus discounts equals actual cost, the retailer pays $\$100,000 - \$8,000 = \$92,000$. Another view of this scenario is that the retailer will pay 92 cents on the dollar. Most retailers will "retail" their goods at the "line price," not including the discount. Thus, the retailer may offer not to credit this discount when vendor analysis, especially in terms of gross margin, is reviewed.

Let us look at another example. A retailer makes a cost purchase of $100,000 with an 8 percent discount. The retailer has an initial markup of 52 percent. With a cost of $100,000, the retail purchase at a 52 percent markup equals $208,333. Assume the retailer achieves sales of $140,000. If this retailer does not credit the manufacturer with the discount, the manufacturer's gross margin would be as follows:

$$
\begin{array}{ll}
\text{Sales} & \$140,000 \\
-\text{ Costs} & \$100,000 \\
\hline
\text{GM\$} & \$\ 40,000
\end{array}
\qquad
\frac{\text{GM}}{\text{Sales}} \quad \frac{40,000}{140,000} = 28.6\ \text{GM\%}
$$

But, this is a faulty comparison. The retailer did not pay $100,000; it paid $92,000. So the astute vendor would request that the GM percentage be recalculated as follows:

$$
\begin{array}{ll}
\text{Sales} & \$140,000 \\
-\text{ Costs} & \$\ 92,000 \\
\hline
\text{GM\$} & \$\ 48,000
\end{array}
$$

$$
\frac{\text{GM}}{\text{Sales}} \quad \frac{\$\ 48,000}{\$140,000} = 34.3\ \text{GM\%}
$$

This is a sizeable increase in gross margin dollars and percentage. Therefore, manufacturers should be very vigilant in checking that discounts given to retailers are properly credited in the profitability analysis. The manufacturer should check that the vendor's gross margin is correctly calculated, so that the retailer does not project a lower gross margin for the manufacturer and try to gain an advantage in future negotiations.

ADJUSTING THE RETAILER'S INITIAL MARKUP

Another method of calculating the correct cost is by using the "discount formula" in conjunction with the initial markup of the retailer. The formula is:

Correct cost =

Initial markup + (Discount × complement of initial markup)

If this formula is applied to the scenario described in the previous section, note the following:

Cost purchases = $100,000

Initial markup = 52%

Retail purchases = $208,333

The retailer achieved sales of $140,000.

1. Convert IMU using the discount formula:

   .52 + (.08 × .48)

   .52 + .0384 = .5584 = 55.84%

2. Take the total retail purchase of $208,333 and determine the true cost using the converted initial markup.

   Retail × complement of markup = Cost

   $208,333 × 44.16% = $92,000

So, the true cost is $92,000, the same as with the method used earlier. The retail mathematician should be familiar with both methods of finding true cost when discounts are involved.

EXERCISES

1. A retailer purchases $63,000 at cost with a discount of 5 percent and an initial markup of 50.5 percent, resulting in a retail purchase of $127,273. After the season ends, the retailer has a total sales figure of $90,000.

    a. Find the gross margin percentage without including the discount.

    b. Find the gross margin percentage including the discount.

2. A major retailer has a gross margin performance arrangement with a designer handbag manufacturer. The manufacturer has agreed to a gross margin that is 3 points (3 percent) better than the retailer's actual gross margin for the entire department. The retailer placed a $200,000 order at retail; the IMU is 53 percent. At the end of the season, the handbag manufacturer's profitability report was as follows: total sales: $150,000; MD: 33.33 percent. The retailer had a departmental gross margin of 37 percent. What is the manufacturer's shortfall dollar amount for the gross margin dollar cost?

3. A retailer makes cost purchases of $150,000. The initial markup is 55 percent, so the retail purchases will be $333,333. The retailer received a 3 percent discount. The retailer's total sales amount was $263,333.

   a. Find the actual gross margin percentage including the discount.

   b. Once you obtain the actual GM percentage, use the maintained markup formula, with a discount-adjusted initial markup percentage, to prove your answer. Hint: You will need to determine the markdown percentage.

4. Following is a flow chart for a major retail chain in the United States.

	January	February	March
BOM	162,000	181,000	198,250
− Sales	35,000	45,250	31,500
− MD	6,000	14,000	9,500
Total handled	121,000	121,750	157,250
+ New receipts	60,000	76,500	43,500
EOM	181,000	198,250	200,750
Turn			

The retailer works on a 52 percent initial markup. For each month, calculate MD percentage, GM percentage, and turn.

	MD%	GM%	Turn
January			
February			
March			

5. Complete the vendor analysis report card in the flow chart that follows, and determine:

    a. Average departmental gross margin percentage

    b. If a buyer received $410,000 at cost for a new season, how should the buyer distribute cost purchases?

IMU = 52%

Vendor	Cost Spent	Retail Sales	GM%	% of OTB	% of Sales
A	30,000	50,000			
B	110,000	170,000			
C	40,000	50,000			
D	20,000	36,000			
E	150,000	210,000			
F	60,000	110,000			
Total					

6. A retailer made a $140,000 purchase at retail from a large manufacturer of coats. The coat department has an initial markup of 52 percent and a season markdown plan of 25 percent. At the end of the season, the actual markdown obtained by the manufacturer was 28 percent. The retailer is asking the manufacturer for $2,625. Is the retailer's markdown dollar request accurate?

7. Questions a–c that follow are based on the following data. The Leslie Group of retailers was evaluating its profitability with select bed frame suppliers. The retailer works on an IMU of 50.5 percent and a markdown plan of 28 percent. A key supplier, ABC Bed Frames, posted the following actual figures for the fall season:

Purchases at cost = $210,000
Discount to Leslie Group: 3%
Actual MMU: 34.7% (not including discount)

a. Leslie Group states that ABC Bed Frames' actual markdowns far exceeded the planned 28 percent. What was the MD percentage for ABC Bed Frames?

b. What is the retailer's IMU if the discount is included?

c. What is Leslie Group's actual cost?

8. Johnny Bob Store places an order with a manufacturer for $23,500 retail. The initial markup is 50 percent and the discount is 2 percent. If everything purchased is shipped, what is Johnny Bob's true cost?

9. Find the markdown percentage if the IMU is 52 percent and the MMU is 40 percent.

10. A retailer made a purchase of $120,000. The retailer plans a markdown of 25 percent. What total sales figure does the retailer need to achieve?

11. A retailer posts the following figures. Determine the total value of the retail purchase that produced this data.

$$Net\ sales = \$80,000$$
$$GM\$ = \$30,000$$
$$IMU = 48\%$$

12. A retailer, with an IMU of 52.5 percent, placed an order for $18,000 at retail. This retailer also received a 4 percent discount. If all product is shipped, determine the retailer's true cost.

13. A retailer purchases $108,695 at retail, with a discount of 8 percent. The initial markup is 54 percent. After the season is over, the retailer finds that this manufacturer's profitability report card shows markdowns of 25 percent. The retailer claims that the manufacturer fell below the gross margin agreement, as the contract provided for a 46 percent gross margin guarantee. The retailer explains the deficit gross margin as follows:

a. To find sales, retail purchases are divided by 1 + the markdown percentage (expressed as a decimal). Thus,

$$\frac{\$108,695}{1.25} = \$86,956$$

b. To find gross margin, subtract costs from sales. Thus,

	Sales	$86,956
−	Costs	$50,000
	GM$	$36,956

c. $\dfrac{GM}{Sales} = GM\%$

$$\frac{\$36,956}{\$86,956} = 42.5 \ GM\% \ \text{(which is less than the agreement)}$$

Is the retailer's calculation of gross margin correct? If not, then why not?

PROJECTS

1. Explain why comparing actual versus planned markdown percentages may not be an accurate measurement of vendor profitability.

2. Explain how discounts given to retailers can impact the profitability performance of a manufacturer.

CHAPTER 5 / Negotiation

It is important to view the tactics of negotiation from the vantage points of the different issues and parties involved. Both the retailer and manufacturer have objectives they need to achieve. The skilled negotiator will have polite and calm demeanor, a professional attitude regarding the presentation of facts supporting any claims, a full understanding of the mathematics involved, and a firmness that is tempered by the ability to make concessions. At the same time, the skilled negotiator must remember that beyond a certain point, the only alternative is to sever the relationship.

This chapter discusses the intricacies of the deal, focusing on the fundamental goals of both retailer and manufacturer. It presents some of the rules of engagement used by two top negotiators in the ready-to-wear industry. No matter how many thousands of dollars a retailer purchases from a vendor, at some point, the markdowns and charge backs may outweigh the advisability of continuing the relationship.

Some retailers and manufacturers feel that once an agreement is made, compliance really needs no negotiation. In other words, if a gross margin agreement is made between a buyer and vendor, the results are not negotiable. If, for example, the manufacturer has missed its gross margin goal, there is nothing to discuss. The manufacturer must make a monetary payment to the retailer. However, such an attitude of total compliance is indicative of a weak negotiator. Giving the other party exactly what they want requires no skill. But a truly skilled negotiator can still gain some ground, even if the outcome is seemingly preordained. A manufacturer may in fact owe a retailer a sum of money, but the manufacturer still may be able to negotiate time of payment, possible installments, non-monetary remuneration, special deals, a minimum purchase guarantee by the vendor, and so on.

Remember that almost any situation leaves some room for negotiation. The exceptions to this rule for the retailer occur when a manufacturer is not considered capable of achieving the gross margin required. Even if large sums of markdown money are given, it will not cure the inherent problem of this vendor not producing a profit. A manufacturer that does business with a retailer that is no longer producing a profit for the manufacturer will become intolerant of the retailer. That point is when charge backs and other monetary demands make it impractical for the manufacturer to continue selling to that retailer. More often than not it is the retailer, serving as the source or outlet for consumer purchases, that sounds the siren of unprofitability.

The retailer must determine how far a particular vendor can be "pushed" (made to accede to demands). To make this determination, the retailer should first measure the store's ability to replace the loss of retail sales revenue if relations with the vendor are discontinued or purchases drastically reduced. If a retail buyer feels reasonably certain that the unprofitable vendor's portion of its total sales goal can be replaced by similar product, the retailer has leverage on a key point of negotiation.

A retailer should also consider the impact of the possible loss of a manufacturer's "label" (popular brand name product) from the store. In rare instances, a retailer will accept a degree of low profit or no profitability just to retain a particular manufacturer's brand name. Once the buyer is confident about being able to replace the loss of sales, the buyer can use the strongest measures available in negotiating with the vendor.

If, as often happens, a vendor's product did not sell to customers, the retailer is left with unsold product—or even more seriously, product sold but not at a profit—and therefore lacks the gross margin dollars that are necessary to do business. At this point, the retail buyer can engage in a two-pronged attack. First, the retailer can ask to return any unsold product to the vendor. Second, the retailer can demand markdown money to help reduce the loss of profit. The retailer can make these demands unconditional by specifying that either the vendor accepts these stipulations or the retailer will sever their relationship.

Although a skilled negotiator may detail many alternatives for the vendor, the threat of discontinuing business makes the vendor the underdog. If, however, the vendor complies with all requests, the relationship remains intact and business should continue. On occasion, however, even after the manufacturer fully complies with the retailer's requests, the retailer, having already returned the unsold product and received the monetary reimbursement, will renege and not make any further purchases. The manufacturer is left feeling violated. There is no legal mechanism to force the retailer to resume purchases from the vendor. Unless the two parties had agreed on a contract, manufacturers seldom pursue legal action when retailers violate the promise of continued business or even when the retailers cancel legal purchase order contracts for a product. If a manufacturer files suit against a retailer, all other businesses will hesitate before making any purchases from that vendor.

Thus, when a manufacturer agrees to supply markdown money to a retailer, the vendor should not write a check, but should make arrangements for the retailer to take a charge back for the amount due from future purchases. This helps strengthen the manufacturer's position because the retailer is forced to continue business in order to deduct the markdown allowance. Of course, if the retailer has not yet paid all of the manufacturer's invoices, the deduction can be applied to those invoices. In that case, the retailer has the freedom to decide not to make further purchases from that vendor.

Often a retail buyer will send a hold payment order into the **accounts payable** department. This protects the retailer by stopping payment to a vendor until claims are deducted from the invoice total. This policy is applied particularly to new vendors, not only because of the potential for markdown money, but also to be certain that the product received is acceptable to the buyer.

NEGOTIATING TACTICS FOR A MANUFACTURER WHEN NO GUARANTEES HAVE BEEN FORMULATED WITH THE RETAILER

The introduction of a manufacturer's line for a new season usually generates considerable excitement. The sales representatives are eager to show and sell their wares during "market week." An enthusiastic salesperson who enters the showroom to greet his or her buyer is often surprised when the buyer's first words are, "We have a problem." Those four words can immediately burst the vendor's bubble of excitement. Of greater importance is the fact that if the buyer's exclamation has the desired effect on the vendor, then the buyer has won the first round because the manufacturer is now instantly on the defensive!

A sales representative who has contact with all of his or her buyers throughout the entire year can usually avoid this situation because the problem of poor retail performance does not occur overnight. If the vendor had communicated with the retailer on a regular basis, the vendor would have been aware of the problem and action could have been taken before the market week appointment. That way, excitement for the new line would not be dampened. If a vendor is surprised to hear that its product is not retailing successfully to the consumer, it is because the vendor was negligent in following up and checking the sales figures at intervals during the selling season. It is always beneficial to address problems before a buyer/vendor showroom appointment so that the meeting can focus on the new product and not involve confrontation or negotiation.

What should a negligent vendor representative do, however, when the retailer suddenly breaks the news of poor sales? First and foremost, the representative should stay calm and allow the wave of disappointment to wash away. The buyer will note the representative's equanimity and not brandish the news as a weapon. As the buyer explains the lack-of-profitability report, the representative should take enough notes so that he or she can explain the salient points to his or her sales manager or any other concerned person. It is critical that the vendor representative determine whether the basis of the retailer's claim of unprofitability is based on the planned or actual gross margin percentage. A conscientious representative should inquire on a regular basis about actual gross margin percentage to determine whether the vendor's achieved gross margin percentage is on or near the retailer's true gross margin.

For example, the men's coat department may have a planned gross margin of 40 percent for the fall season. Because of warm weather, however, the actual achieved gross margin from all vendors was only 35 percent for the season. Upon inquiry, our vendor learns that its actual gross margin was 36 percent for the season. Thus, although the vendor is deficient, it did in fact beat the average actual gross margin. It is possible that no vendor reached the planned margin.

Should individual vendors be held to a planned percentage when retailers could not manage to reach their own goals from the aggregate of all their vendors? In the case of the coat department, the retailer used a standard that was impossible to achieve in an unexpectedly warm winter. As a result, all vendors were penalized. The vendor should strongly protest these expectations because the planned gross margin percentage proved unrealistic.

A much more serious situation occurs when the vendor's gross margin is substantially lower than the retailer's actual gross margin. In this case, buyers will be persistent in seeking compensation. Manufacturers will see the possibility of having to accept returns of out-of-season merchandise. The buyer will push for closure by demanding that the manufacturer grant markdown requests. Sales representatives must stand strong and not agree to grant money when first asked. There are two reasons for this refusal. First, the vendor needs time to review and substantiate the numbers. If the manufacturer is familiar with the principles of profitability analysis, he will be able to determine whether the retailer's request is accurate. Second, delay may create a psychological advantage for the manufacturer. With the passage of time, the retailer may lower some of its demands in an effort to gain closure. In some instances, if the retailer has received enough markdown dollars from other vendors that conceded immediately, the demands on more resistant vendors may lessen.

The main goal of a manufacturer's appointment time with a buyer is to sell product. However, some buyers may refuse to view the new line until the current shortfalls are addressed. This can certainly create a dilemma. To placate the buyer, the manufacturer should remind the buyer that as a partner, the manufacturer has every intention of satisfying the buyer, but that it is policy to review any markdown requests. A manufacturer that can derail the buyer who expects an immediate response should be considered an excellent negotiator. A manufacturer also must accurately judge the buyer's response to a line presentation by looking for any hints as to whether the buyer plans future purchases. If a retailer does not plan to make purchases from a particular vendor, then markdown requests may become a moot issue.

Once the buyer has acquiesced to giving the manufacturer time to absorb the profitability analysis request, an agreement should be concluded to guarantee that the retailer will continue the relationship. The manufacturer should try to link the expected markdown contribution to the impending order for product because the manufacturer's decision on the markdown allowance is often predicated on the monetary value of the buyer's order. This is true because many vendors allow for a specific percentage of sales as possible charge back allowances.

For example, a manufacturer has achieved a $100,000 sales volume with a retailer during a year. If the agreement specifies 3 percent of sales as a possible charge back, the manufacturer knows that $3,000 (3 percent of $100,000) is available for the buyer. Thus, if the manufacturer is pressured to provide markdown money, it will be more flexible with the knowledge of substantial future orders from the retailer, and negotiations could proceed along these lines. Markdown money that is legitimately requested can be authorized as long as the retailer's sales-to-charge-backs ratio is in line with the specified percentage. Most manufacturers will cushion their markup percentage by including this money for this potential markdown request.

Only employees with authorization from management should conduct negotiations. Following is a list of steps that you, as a vendor representative, can use to negotiate with retailers when no pre-existing deal is in place:

1. Use the skills learned in vendor analysis and confirm the accuracy of the retailer's profitability report.
2. Discuss any discrepancies noted.
3. Before making any decision, tell the buyer you must review the reports with your management.

4. Determine whether the buyer's figures are based on planned or actual calculations.

5. Fight for your company.

INSIDE SCOOP

Perspectives on Negotiating Gross Margin Agreements

Vendor: Colleen Kelly
Colleen Kelly is president of Calvin Klein Jeans.

In the world of department stores, the key to success is no longer having product that retails (although it certainly helps). The vendors with the deepest pockets have taken over the real estate in most of these stores. Department stores have little space left to test new resources that cannot contribute end-of-the-season gross margins dollars. I have had the opportunity to work for both types of manufacturers—those with a lot of capital and those without. Many smaller companies have reached a plateau, with little or no potential for growth, because growth requires a solid gross margin guarantee that, in many stores, needs to be paid quarterly—and sometimes, even monthly. Department store managers know that they need to grow a resource with little or no risk to their profitability. A small company cannot afford to commit to these payments because one bad season could mean the end of the business itself. Small businesses need to be cautious, so they limit the number of doors (retail outlets) they are in, thereby limiting their liability. It is only a matter of time before a vendor with more capital will ask for more square footage in that door and the little vendor will disappear.

It may seem as if the large vendors have an easier time. That was certainly my expectation when arriving at a large company. I soon discovered, however, that it is even difficult for a large vendor to be profitable with the gross margin requirements that are in place in many departments. For example, if a vendor has an initial markup of 52 percent and has a gross margin guarantee of 42 percent, the vendor starts losing money as soon as the markdown rises above 21 percent. I have not seen that low a markdown rate in the history of my career! In some cases, the payment can be up to 30 percent of the wholesaler's cost of the shipment.

The greatest challenge is to determine how much markdown money can be contributed on an annual basis to keep the retailer satisfied and the vendor in business. Manufacturers work on different internal markups. Those with higher markups may be able to afford more markdown money. Other vendors may consider raising their wholesale prices to build in a markdown money cushion. One needs to be careful with this strategy, as higher prices may cause an item not to sell, thereby creating more markdowns.

It may appear that all of the control is in the retailer's hands, but the vendor can control many aspects of the business in an effort to ensure a fair partnership. Before entering into an agreement, the following points should be negotiated:

1. The vendor needs to have final approval over the assortment that is purchased. After all, if they are paying the markdowns, they should feel confident that the top-performing items are in the store.

2. The vendor should know and approve in advance of each season the space in which they will be housed—both the location and the square footage.

3. The vendor should know what level of staffing to expect in the store for their merchandise in terms of sales and sales support.

4. The vendor has the right to expect that markdowns will be taken on time and signed properly to ensure maximum exposure.

5. The vendor has a right to discuss seasonal and annual receipt plans with the retailer in advance of the actual buys. The expectation with a gross margin guarantee is that business should, at a minimum, grow in line with the department average. If the vendor's product is performing extremely well, additional receipts and doors can be discussed.

6. The vendor has a right to receive, on time, weekly and seasonal selling results by account, by door, and by style. This information can tell a vendor very quickly how she is performing and what kind of payout will be needed at season's end. These reports can also allow a vendor to react before the season's end to fix any problems. She may opt to take merchandise back or swap into better sellers.

A solid partnership between the retailer and vendor can develop if all aspects of the agreement are discussed in depth and agreed to mutually. Nothing should be left for interpretation at the end of the season. One needs to make sure which factors are included in the gross margin calculation. Pure vendor margin excludes shortage, workroom costs, freight, and employee discounts. Gross margin usually includes all of the above factors, which can cost an additional 5 to 6 percent in some cases. The agreement must specify clearly what is and what is not included. All of this can be negotiated, as long as it is negotiated up front.

If, during the course of the season, any one of the above points are not adhered to, there needs to be immediate communication. If, for example, merchandise is moved to a less desirable location, a sale was not properly signed, the selling staff is significantly reduced, or a large purchase order was canceled, there are grounds for reducing the end-of-season payment. One needs to evaluate the loss in sales caused by the change and speak to management about how this will impact the season end contribution. One cannot reduce the end-of-season payment without proper advance notification and documentation. The retailer needs an opportunity to make changes if she is not getting all of the money anticipated for that season.

Another example occurred when a stockperson was released by a retailer because of layoffs in the department. As a result, our merchandise remained in the stockroom, unopened for several weeks. As soon as I was informed of this, I contacted store management and told them how many dollars in sales I believed had been lost during that time period. I informed them that I was going to include that loss in the gross margin calculations. The next day, five employees were assigned to unpack our boxes. This is proof that the vendor has some leverage.

When settling the gross margin agreement at the end of the season, check and double check all of the components included in the calculation. In many cases, the buyer simply puts numbers into a template. Mistakes are often made—rarely to the benefit of the vendor. Note that calculating out to two decimal points can save money if a very large dollar amount is in question.

The most important thing to remember is that the relationship between the vendor and the retailer needs to be a true partnership. Both should have equal responsibility for the success of the brand. If either side gains more control, it will eventually result in declining sales. We all need to focus on the shared goal of selling merchandise at the regular price. The strategic plan should address how to accomplish that end. If success is achieved, then the gross margin agreement becomes only a security blanket.

Retailer: Elly Christophersen
Elly Christophersen is a retail buyer for a major chain.

The keys to effective negotiations are knowledge of the facts, a well-prepared game plan, and execution of that plan.

KNOW YOUR FACTS

Before entering into negotiations, a retailer should know the target retail amount, how much she can pay for the merchandise, and what price (both retail and cost) the market will bear. The retailer should also learn certain facts about the manufacturer's product, including the current retail pricing structure, promotional activities, and what other retailers carry the product.

DEVELOP A GAME PLAN

The retailer needs a careful strategy for communicating her needs. During negotiations, the retailer needs to:

1. Confirm that the manufacturer understands the retailer's needs, even if there is some disagreement about them.

2. Anticipate how the manufacturer will respond to requests.

3. Recall past negotiations: what transpired and how problems were resolved.

4. Set up an appointment that allows time for negotiating and create an atmosphere that allows for give and take. Try to acquire a sense of the "mood" or state of mind of the manufacturer—and observe body language carefully. If the "vibes" are negative, reschedule.

5. Be consistent and reinforce the store's needs repeatedly.

EXECUTION

You can achieve more positive results with an optimistic, energetic, and friendly approach to negotiations, especially if profit margins are at risk. Be sure to give the manufacturer plenty of time to speak. An overwhelming negotiator rarely gets positive results. Remember a deal that does not happen one day may happen the next. Be in touch with manufacturers and stay persistent.

RENEGOTIATING A PREEXISTING DEAL

When a retail buyer presents a profitability report to a vendor who has failed to meet the expected goals, the retailer's standard argument usually sounds like this: "Our gross margin agreement was for 42 percent. Your actual gross margin was 38 percent. I have calculated the difference to be $7,000." The percentages and markdown dollar requests vary from case to case, but, whatever the amounts involved, the vendor should not assume that there is no room to maneuver.

Even in these situations, the vendor should try to gain some considerations. Operating under the axiom "you must give to get," the vendor's negotiator should consider the following list of possible concessions from the retailer:

1. The vendor will pay the markdown amount in an installment plan based on charge backs.

2. The partnership will continue, with the retailer increasing purchases.

3. The markdown amount should be distributed in the following fashion:

   One-third cash (charge backs)

   One-third discounts on future purchases

   One-third special off price merchandise so the retailer will enjoy higher margins

4. The vendor may state that the markdown requests are at retail. The actual amount should be the cost equivalent of the retailer's initial markup percentage.

5. Elimination of or a decrease in the retailer's charge backs for the following:

   shortages

   employee discounts

   workroom costs

6. Verification that all discounts, markdowns, and allowances are included in the profitability report.

THE MANUFACTURER'S LAMENT

Most manufacturers are not well versed in retail analysis and can be easily intimidated by a buyer equipped with computer printouts. Therefore, many manufacturers do not dispute the merits of the request, only the amount itself. If a retailer asks for $10,000 in markdown allowance, the vendor will arbitrarily offer $5,000.

Remember, because buyers also know how many vendors work, the wise buyer, who only requires $5,000, will request $10,000. The vendor who agrees relaxes in a sea of lower profits. Do not be gullible when negotiating.

THE "KING'S GAMBIT"

The phrase "King's Gambit" is based on a strategy in the game of chess. When applied to retail mathematics, it means that the manufacturer who is presented with a retailer's profitability report showing a poor performance should keep the following goals clearly in mind:

1. Reducing markdown requests by skillfully augmenting dollar requests with special deals to increase profitability in the future
2. Cementing the relationship by leaving the negotiator's table with an order for future product

Examine very carefully any analysis presented in the form of monthly statistics. Retailers commonly include markdowns for a month that was previously included in a markdown allowance. For example, a retailer may list huge markdowns for a certain month. The month in question, however, was originally addressed in a previous markdown allowance.

Decisions based on the potential of future profits should enter into the negotiating equation. Before negotiations begin, a vendor must determine the break-away point. If negotiations reach this point, the vendor has already determined that the relationship will end. Always make certain that management has approved negotiating tactics, as an error can be costly. A negotiator must never exceed the limits of his or her position and authority.

EXERCISES

1. A manufacturer of greeting cards is reviewing its profitability
    with a supplier, the Chism Card Corporation. Chism had no
    agreement or profitability arrangements with the retailer. The
    retailer presented the following data:

    Profitability Report

    "Chism"

    Retail purchases = $42,500

    Terms of sale = Net 10 Days

    IMU = 56%

    Actual GM = 40% (including reductions listed below)

    Employee discounts = 2% ⎤

    Shortages = 2% ⎬ Reductions

    Workroom costs = 2% ⎦

    Planned department GM = 42%

    According to this report, the vendor's gross margin is defi-
    cient and requires compensation. If you represented the Chism
    Card Corporation, detail your negotiation tactics.

2. A large shoe retail chain is discussing its seasonal profitability with Jones and Smith Shoe Manufacturers as follows:

Vendor = Jones and Smith

Season = Fall

IMU = 60%

Markdowns = 40%

The shoe retailer is disturbed by the high markdown percentage. How might a representative of the Jones and Smith company combat the retailer's observation?

3. After a particularly poor season, a housewares manufacturer owes a retailer $100,000 in markdown money. The retailer asks the manufacturer for a check in the proper amount. As the negotiator for the housewares manufacturer, detail your response.

4. A sweater manufacturer with a deficient profitability report from one of its retail store clients is trying to determine options for compensation other than money. Compile a list of suggestions.

5. A bedding manufacturer receives jubilant news as to its profitability for the past season. The manufacturer posted honors as the most profitable gross margin in the department. Assume you are the representative for the bedding manufacturer. How would you use the above information to your benefit?

6. A retail buyer ended her season with the following profitability report from a key vendor:

Retail purchases = $110,000

IMU = 54.5%

Planned MD = 32.0%

Actual MD = 34.5%

How much money does this buyer need to reach her planned profit? Use gross margin as the standard for determining profitability.

Questions 7 through 10 are based on the following profitability reports presented to a manufacturer. In each case, the manufacturer has failed to reach the agreed-upon profitability. Determine, from the manufacturer's perspective, how much money is owed and how you might negotiate terms other than payment of the sum requested. Use gross margin as the standard for determining profitability.

7. Retail purchases = $150,000

IMU = 52%

Planned markdown = 26%

Actual markdown = 30%

8.   Retail purchases = $220,000

                    IMU = 54%

                Discount =   8%

    Planned markdown = 25%

      Actual markdown = 29%

9.   Retail purchases = $80,000

                    IMU = 48%

    Planned gross margin = 40%

      Actual gross margin = 37%

10.   Retail purchases = $180,000

IMU = 53.5%

Actual sales = $123,000

Planned gross margin = 40%

11. A retailer in the Midwest had a poor season because of severe snowstorms that forced him to frequently close the store. Of course, manufacturers' sales reflected this difficulty. Many manufacturers had high gross margin agreements, as they never anticipated such inclement weather. Now, the retailer is asking manufacturers to pay profitability money. Write a short essay on the ramifications of the retailer's request.

PROJECTS

1. Below are five profitability reports from a large retail chain. For each report, two students or two teams of students should take turns negotiating the best possible deal from the perspective of the retailer or the manufacturer. The retailers should press for as much monetary compensation as they think necessary to reach their profit projections. The manufacturers should negotiate the best deal possible. Teams should mediate the following issues:

   a. performance of profitability based on gross margin

   b. whether there is a shortfall of profit that needs to be addressed

   c. how much, if anything, is the deficit amount

      I. Vendor ABC

         Retail purchases = $120,000

                  IMU = 52%

         Planned markdowns = 28%

         Actual markdowns = 30%

      II. Vendor DEF

         Retail purchases = $200,000

                  IMU = 53%

         Planned markups = 40%

         Actual markups = 37%

      III. Vendor GHI

         Purchases at cost = $125,000

                  IMU = 52.5%

         Actual markdowns = 30%

         Planned sales = $195,000

      IV. Vendor JKL

         Retail purchases = $150,000

                  IMU = 52%

         Terms of sale = 4% discount

         Planned markdowns = 30%

         Actual markdowns = 32%

V. Vendor MNO

$$\begin{aligned}
\text{Retail purchases} &= \$240{,}000 \\
\text{IMU} &= 50\% \\
\text{Planned gross margin} &= 42\% \\
\text{Actual gross margin} &= 39.5\%
\end{aligned}$$

2. A buyer from a large department store chain tells a vendor that even though the vendor has actually met the gross margin goal by the exact amount, the retailer still needs markdown money compensation. The reason stated is that as a key vendor, the manufacturer should have exceeded the goal, as did other less critical vendors. Discuss the ramifications of this situation from all sides.

CHAPTER 6 / Turn: The Life and Breath of Retail

The profitability of any retail business is, in the last analysis, determined by its "turn." But this most important calculation has more than one formula because turn has more than one meaning.

Most generally, **turn** is the amount of sales per square foot of selling space in a given period of time. The retailer determines how many times during that period items were sold and replaced in the same space. Therefore, turn is the flow rate of merchandising, selling, and replacing sold merchandise. This "turnover" rate, or turn rate, is one of the key figures in a retail store's financial analysis. To calculate turn for an entire department or store, the retailer needs to include all available selling space. An additional—and much more common measurement—is to compare actual sales against the average amount of inventory for sale. Clearly, an increase in the turn rate is extremely desirable.

For example, imagine that the following box represents a square foot in a retail shoe store.

Suppose the retailer places a pair of shoes in that exact space. To determine the turn of that space during a six-month period, the retailer would count how many times a pair of shoes sold in that space, was replaced with a new pair of shoes and sold again. If during a six-month period, three pairs of shoes were sold in that exact space, the retailer had three turns. If the retailer sold four or five pairs of shoes in that exact space during the same period, the turn for that square foot of space would increase.

Because every store has a finite amount of space, there is a physical limit as to how much merchandise or inventory can be displayed for sale at one time. So it is logical that the more swiftly inventory sells, the more often that inventory can be replaced and sold again.

The formula that mathematically expresses this turn or turnover factor is:

$$\frac{X}{1} = \frac{\text{Sales}}{\text{Average inventory}}$$

(with X equal to the turn rate). So far, the proportion expressed in this equation is fairly simple.

Remember that a key factor in implementing the turn formula is the need to know the exact time reference the formula expresses. For example, if inventory turned once and sales were $300,000, average inventory can be calculated as follows:

$$\frac{X}{1} = \frac{\text{Sales}}{\text{Average inventory}} = \frac{1}{1} = \frac{\$300,000}{X}$$
$$X = \$300,000$$

So, **average retail stock** is determined and the retailer knows that:

$$\frac{1}{1} = \frac{\$300,000}{\$300,000}$$

The equation is solved, but to evaluate whether this rate of turn is successful, the element of time must be added to the analysis. Therefore, the example should be restated as follows. If inventory turned one time in a three-month period and sales were $300,000, was the turn ratio a good one? The turn ratio, which is still 1.0, must now be compared to the store's turn plan. If, for example, the turn plan for the months January, February, and March was 0.85, then indeed the actual turn was greater than the planned turn, as turn was 1.0.

THE TURN TIME TABLE

Most retailers receive turn plans based on a six-month buying cycle, but this does not mean that the buyer must—or should—wait six

INSIDE SCOOP

Defining Turn

Elly Christophersen

Elly Christophersen is a retail buyer for a major chain.

While the overall concept of turn is relevant to both retailers and manufacturers, each of them emphasizes different specifics. The retailer is particularly concerned with the daily turn or movement of products through sales. If the planned turn is achieved, it should produce a smooth cash flow, which is necessary for meeting current debt and replacing sold merchandise or products. Constant replenishment of product that is desirable to the consumer is of paramount importance. If a retail store sells product but fails to replace what is sold, sales will take a significant downturn. Remember that if product is sold and not replaced, the store or department will soon suffer an exponential drop in sales.

Ira Lindner

Ira Lindner, a former owner of a men's retail store chain, is currently senior account executive at a major apparel manufacturer.

Manufacturers concern themselves with three aspects of turn. Their first concern parallels that of the retailer, for it is their product that is under scrutiny. The success or failure of the product will be based on how the product sells to the consumer.

The manufacturer, however, is also concerned with how certain functions of financial information are used. The first turn formula details how fast money that is owed is repaid:

$$\text{Accounts receivable turnover} = \frac{\text{Net credit sales}}{\text{Average accounts receivable}}$$

The second formula details the manufacturer's ability to turn over, or sell, its inventory:

$$\text{Inventory turnover} = \frac{\text{Cost of goods sold}}{\text{Average inventory}}$$

months before checking the turn rate. Turn can be calculated for any period of time and provides an interim check on whether goals are being met.

Problem #1

A retail store plans two turns for a six-month period. The sales plan is for $400,000, and the average stock level is $200,000. How would you calculate turn for different periods of time within the six months?

Solution

A good first step is to construct a chart as follows:

Time Span	6 Months	3 Months	1 Month	1 Week
Sales	400,000			
Stock	200,000			
Turn rate	2			

If this chart reflects the rate of turn for six months using $200,000 as the average stock value, then every time span will have $200,000 as its average stock value. If $200,000 is the average stock value for six months, it must also be the average for every other period of time. Thus:

Time Span	6 Months	3 Months	1 Month	1 Week
Sales	400,000			
Stock	200,000	200,000	200,000	200,000
Turn rate				

Next, the different time elements must be converted to adjust sales and turns for other periods. If the turn for six months is two, then in one-half that time, three months, turn must be one-half of two, or one. With this information, the sales for a three-month period can be calculated as follows:

$$1/2 \text{ the time} = 1/2 \text{ the turn}$$

Therefore,

$$3 \ months = \frac{1}{1} = \frac{X}{200,000} = X = 200,000$$

Now, this additional information can be filled in on the chart:

Time Span	6 Months	3 Months	1 Month	1 Week
Sales	400,000	200,000		
Stock	200,000	200,000	200,000	200,000
Turn rate	2	1		

Following this procedure, sales can now be calculated for a one-month period. Once again, find the correct turn time calculation by referring to the information previously provided. If there are two turns in six months, it follows that one-sixth of that amount would be sold in one-sixth that time. Thus we divide two turns by six:

$$\frac{2}{6} = .33 \text{ turn in one month}$$

Now using the turn formula:

$$\frac{.33}{1} = \frac{X}{200,000} = .33 \times \$200,000 = \$66,000$$

The chart now looks like this:

Time Span	6 Months	3 Months	1 Month	1 Week
Sales	400,000	200,000	66,000	
Stock	200,000	200,000	200,000	200,000
Turn rate	2	1	.33	

Now complete the chart by calculating the data for a one-week period. This means two turns in six months or two turns in 26 weeks. Therefore,

$$\frac{2}{26} = .077 \text{ turns in one week}$$

Now that the six-month turn has been converted into its one-week equivalent, the retailer can determine sales as follows:

$$\frac{.077}{1} = \frac{X}{200,000} = .077 \times \$200,000 = \$15,400$$

NOTE: When calculating weekly turn, remember that using monthly turn and dividing by four weeks is not valid because a month actually has 4.25 weeks.

Now the chart can be completed:

Time Span	6 Months	3 Months	1 Month	1 Week
Sales	400,000	200,000	66,000	15,400
Stock	200,000	200,000	200,000	200,000
Turn rate	2	1	.33	.077

Another weekly calculation is to determine sell through. To calculate this percentage, add sales for the week and merchandise on hand. Divide that total by the weekly sales.

USING TURN TO IMPROVE MERCHANDISING

Businesses need to evaluate turn for the proper purchase and merchandising of inventory. A carefully planned retail business bases its sales plan on a maintained "average stock level." Maintaining the desired average stock level depends on the proper calculation of the stock to sales level ratio and on timely shipments from suppliers. A sudden downturn in achieving sales and/or late or canceled orders from its suppliers will adversely affect any retail establishment.

Another factor that can adversely affect the average stock level is a large increase in sales without a corresponding increase in stock. "Turning too quickly" means selling faster than planned and that there is not sufficient inventory in stock to replace sold items promptly. This can seriously deplete existing supplies. In addition, because it is usually the popular items that sell, the retailer is left with a skeleton inventory of the less popular items. Thus, a decrease in planned stock approaching the 15 percent level can result in an exponentially adverse sales level. A retailer's "average stock level" is therefore a key factor, as turn itself is a measure of profitability.

BLOWOUT

Occasionally, both the retailer and the manufacturer experience the joy and excitement of having a "blowout." A blowout occurs when a product is so desired by consumers that the retailer cannot purchase enough to satisfy the demand.

When a blowout does occur, the product is most commonly a toy. For example, if a vendor has one of the most popular toys for the Christmas season, supply cannot always keep up with demand. In merchandising terms, this is known as "turning too quickly." Sales are "lost," as retailers rush to replenish depleted shelf space.

MEASURING PROFITABILITY USING TURN

Assume that for a six-month period sales totaled $300,000 and the average stock level was $150,000 at retail. First, calculate turn as follows:

$$\frac{Turn}{1} = \frac{Sales}{Stock} = \frac{X}{1} = \frac{300,000}{150,000} = 2 \text{ Turns}$$

This equation shows that every dollar spent for "inventory" produces two dollars in sales. Thus, if one of those sales dollars is spent to replenish stock (for proper maintenance of the stock level), one dollar would remain for operating expenses and, hopefully, a profit.

Another example is a retail store with 1.5 turns in six months. Its profits would be evaluated as follows:

$$
\begin{array}{r}
1.5 \text{ turns} \\
- 1.0 \text{ (one dollar to replace depleted stock)} \\
\hline
- 0.5
\end{array}
$$

This means 50 cents of gross profit revenue.

In practice, a turn of two times in a six-month period is extremely difficult to obtain. Few retailers are capable of achieving such a high turn rate. The number of decisions and events that would need to occur simultaneously to achieve a rate of two turns in six months would include a near perfect selection of product highly desired by the consumers, and economic conditions favorable for retail sales.

Retail sales are an important factor in the nation's statistics on economic conditions. Strong retail sales are considered a measure of the consumer's "confidence" in the economy, because retail sales include discretionary purchases of nonessential items that might be considered frivolous in more unstable economic times. Consumers are more likely to purchase items such as toys, clothing, cosmetics, and appliances in a growing economy.

TURN AS A MERCHANDISING TOOL

Another critical merchandising statistic used extensively in retail planning is a sales plan based on turn.

Problem #2

A retailer is constructing a weekly sales plan for the spring season that includes a turn of 1.5 in the six-month period with average stock worth $250,000 at retail. How does turn factor into these calculations?

Solution

STEP I: Use the turn formula to calculate total sales planned for the spring season.

$$\frac{T}{1} = \frac{\text{Sales}}{\text{Stock}}$$

$$\frac{1.5}{1} = \frac{X}{\$250,000} = X = \$375,000$$

Therefore, total sales for the spring season equal $375,000.

STEP II: To find the average weekly sales plan, divide total sales by 26 (26 weeks in 6 months) as follows:

$$\frac{\$375,000}{26 \text{ weeks}} = \$14,423 = \text{average one-week sales}$$

Converting the spring season to an average weekly sale plan allows a buyer to gauge probable success on a weekly basis. If a month passes (some retailers may react even sooner) with deficient sales, stock adjustments can be implemented.

EXERCISES

1. If a retailer's turn rate is .75 and stock is $114,000, determine sales.

2. A retailer plans a six-month turn of 1.75. The sales plan is $160,000. What is the value of the average stock?

3. A retailer plans sales of $400,000 and an average stock level of $200,000 for a six-month period. Find the weekly turn rate.

4. A retailer has an average stock level of $80,000 and a six-month turn of 1.5. Find the weekly average planned sales.

5. A retailer has a monthly turn of 0.25 and an average stock level of $200,000. Find the sales plan for a six-month period.

6. A retailer has a weekly turn rate of 0.075. Its average stock level is $150,000. Find the sales plan for a six-month period.

7. If a retailer has a six-month turn ratio of 1.5 and stock of $300,000, what is the average monthly sales level?

8. If a retailer has an average weekly turn ratio of 0.05, what will its six-month turn rate be?

9. A new, intimate restaurant opened in SoHo in New York City. Its size allows room for only six tables, each able to seat four patrons, but it is usually filled to capacity. The restaurant serves only dinner, from 6 to 10 P.M. nightly. The average cost of a meal per person is $75.00, and the average length of a meal is two hours.

   a. What is the restaurant's average turn per table per night?

   b. If the restaurant cut the average time per meal from 2 hours to 80 minutes, how might income be affected?

10. The staff of a major retail store was discussing the previous season's profitability for the Better Dress Department. The General merchandise manager said, "Our average inventory for the past six months has been $400,000, and our six-month sales totaled $500,000 for the same period." The GMM then added, "For each dollar in inventory we earned only 25 cents gross profit." Explain the GMM's statement.

11. A retailer planned a turn rate of 1.5 for six months. After the first month this retailer posted the following:

January
Sales = $35,000
BOM = $120,000
EOM = $140,000

Does the turn rate for the first month indicate that the six-month turn rate will be met or exceeded?

12. A retail buyer, in checking her sales for last week, noted the following:

Sales for week = $40,000
On hand = $360,000

What was the weekly percent sell through?

PROJECTS

1. Explain why the retail-sales-per-square-foot formula is so important.

2. A movie theater has a 200-seat capacity and is currently playing to a full house for each performance. What might the theater owner consider to increase daily sales if ticket prices cannot be increased?

3. Complete the chart below based on the following information. In addition, explain the gross profit obtained in the six-month period.

	1 Week	1 Month	3 Months	6 Months
Sales	$10,000			
Stock				
Turn	0.1			

In the early twentieth century, most retail stores still used the cost method of inventory, by which the gross margin dollars were divided by the cost of the merchandise sold. Then in the 1920s, particularly in the United States, the retail method was implemented. This new method offered convenience in maintaining inventory records and offered tax advantages. This method compares all components of profit (i.e., cost of goods sold, gross margin, and profit or loss) to the retail (sales) price. This method is still taught to and used by retailers in the United States, but most other countries use the cost method.

COMPARISON OF THE RETAIL VERSUS THE COST METHOD OF MARKUP

It is generally accepted that when any number is doubled, it increases 100 percent. This is true in every branch of mathematics except the retail method of determining markup, as will be shown shortly.

Cost Method

The cost method, which is still used in Europe, Asia, and South America, uses the following formula:

Retail price
$$\frac{-\text{ Cost price}}{\text{MU\$}}$$

Retail price	=	$100
− Cost price	=	$ 50
MU$	=	$ 50

Then, the markup dollars are divided by the cost amount. Thus,

---

CLOSING THE LANES

Many manufacturers are now doing business in a global marketplace. Both manufacturers and outlet stores dotted across the globe need to communicate business data accurately and effectively to one another. In my role as retail analyst for a number of major fashion houses, I am amazed by the lack of expertise among employees about how to communicate and interpret data.

For example, a shoe manufacturer exporting from Milan will be schooled in the cost method of markup, while the buyer in the United States may—or may not—be aware of the ramifications of the differences in markup systems. A shoe that costs $120 and is retailed for $264 produces a gross margin of $144. This is always true, but the routes for calculating the markup are different.

This is another example of an industry-wide problem, which is the lack of understanding of many elementary financial concepts.

$$\frac{\text{MU\$} = \$50}{\text{Cost dollars} = \$50} = 1 \text{ or } 100\%$$

Thus, if the cost method of retail is used, the mathematical principle stated earlier is true. If you double the cost price, the result is a 100 percent increase.

Problem #1

Find the markup percentage using the cost method of inventory if the retail price is $400 and the cost price is $200.

Solution

First, determine the markup dollars by subtracting the cost price from the retail price. Thus,

$$\$400 - \$200 = \$200 \text{ MU}$$

Then, divide the markup percentage by the retail price:

$$\frac{\$200}{\$200} = 100\% \text{ MU}$$

Retail Method

In the retail method, used primarily in the United States, any cost that is doubled has only a 50 percent markup because the markup dollar amount is divided by the retail price rather than by the cost price.

Retail price	=	$100
− Cost price	=	$ 50
MU$	=	$ 50

The markup dollars are then divided by the retail price to determine the markup percentage. Thus,

$$\frac{\text{MU\$} = \$ 50}{\text{Retail dollars} = \$100} = 0.5 \text{ or } 50\%$$

Because two different methods of costing may be used, many retailers and manufacturers that buy and sell internationally must be careful about drawing incorrect references from the available data. A retail store in the United States would state that its markup percentage goal is 50 percent, while a retail store in Europe selling the exact same item at the exact same cost and retail would state that the markup percentage goal is 100 percent. So these two stores would be using different numbers to say the exact same thing. Thus, if a chain of retail stores in the United States and a rival chain in South America were not aware of the different systems of computing markup percentage, neither would correctly interpret the data from the other.

For example, a shoe store in the United States purchases a particular style of shoes at $75 per pair and retails them for $165 per pair. This is a markup percentage of 54.55 using the retail method. However, in Europe the markup would be cost multiplied by 2.2 for a total of $165. (The actual cost percentage of markup is 120 percent, or 1.2. When marking up using the cost method, you add "1" for the complement. Thus the cost is multiplied by 2.2).

Problem #2

Find the markup percentage using the retail method of inventory if the retail price is $400 and the cost price is $200.

Solution

First determine the markup dollars by subtracting the cost price from the retail price. Thus,

$$\$400 - \$200 = \$200 \text{ MU}$$

Then, divide markup dollars by the retail price:

$$\frac{\$200}{\$400} = 50\% \text{ MU}$$

COST VALUES OF ASSETS

Although the United States uses the retail method of inventory, one of the key elements of a financial statement—the balance sheet—replaces the retail method of inventory with the cost value of assets.

Why? Because it would be extremely difficult to determine the retail value of unsold inventory; you cannot accurately predict the price at which it might sell at some future date. Often, even the cost is overstated. For example, if a buyer makes an unwise purchase of an unwanted item, the cost worth will be difficult to determine in the marketplace.

Turn, or turn rate, gives the retail analyst a key component for evaluating a business—the "gross margin return on investment." Whether turn will remain as a key component remains to be seen. Traditionally, the benchmark of success is for a retailer to turn inventory twice in six months (four times per year), but the future may create a new standard of retailing. The retail store is becoming a dinosaur as on-line shopping and the renewed popularity of ordering by mail through catalogs replaces the physical store. What will occupy the space now dominated by retail stores?

Alas, evolution!

CONVERSION FROM ONE METHOD TO ANOTHER

Once the cost and retail amounts are known, it is easy to convert to either the retail or cost method of markup.

Cost Method to Retail Method

A European buyer, with a cost method markup percentage of 1.4 (140%), asks that this percentage be used to sell products in the United States. The American buyer should first calculate the equivalent markup as determined by the retail method. To do so, the U.S. buyer first chooses random cost and applies the foreign markup. Thus,

$$\text{Random cost of } \$100 \times \text{foreign markup of } 1.4 = \$140$$

With this information, the U.S. buyer now determines the retail cost of markup as follows:

$$
\begin{aligned}
\text{Retail} &= \$140 \\
- \text{Cost} &= \$100 \\
\hline
& \$40
\end{aligned}
$$

$$\frac{\$40}{\$140} = 28.6\% \text{ MU}$$

In the retail method, cost divided by the complement of markup percentage yields the retail price. For this example, $100 divided by .714 (the complement of the 28.6 percent markup percentage) produces the $140 retail price. In the cost method, that same retail price was obtained by multiplying the cost by 1.4 or 140%.

$$\text{Cost } \$100 \times 1.4 = \$140$$

Retail Method to Cost Method

This calculation requires additional steps. Assume that a European buyer wants to convert a retail markup of 52 percent to its cost markup equivalent. As with the previous example, the buyer must first choose a random cost. Then the buyer must calculate the retail price as follows:

$$\frac{\text{Cost of } \$100}{48\% \text{ (complement of 52\% markup used in the retail method)}} = \text{Retail price of } \$208.33$$

Thus,

Retail price of $208.33 less the Cost of $100 = Markup $108.33

To determine the cost markup, divide markup dollars by the cost as follows:

$$\frac{\$108.33}{\$100} = 1.0833$$

For this cost markup to be used, "1" must be added to the cost:

Cost Markup Obtained $1.0833 + 1 = 2.0833$

The number "1" is added to the calculation to create a reciprocal, or complementary, value. This minimizes the number of steps in the calculation and is similar to the retail method of inventory, which uses the formula:

Cost $\times$ complement of markup %

Now, confirm the retail price using this cost markup:

Cost of $100 $\times$ 2.0833 = Retail price of $208.33

INSIDE SCOOP

On-Line Retailing

In 2001, 4 percent of retail sales were made on-line; by 2002, this number had grown to 10 percent of all retail sales. In addition, as technology improves, the buyer can do more than just pick from an on-line catalog; the buyer can view products, such as clothing, in virtual reality environments that show actual texture, fabric, quality, and fit in three-dimensional images that move and turn so that the flow of the garment can be simulated.

Thus, as the Internet increasingly takes sales away from retail stores, the impact on the concept of turn must be re-examined. Because all retail stores have a finite size, an increase in turn within the same space results in an increase in sales. The calculation of sales volume per square foot of space has always been a key element in planning a business, but will that calculation be as important in the future?

With on-line shopping, floor space is not an issue; nor are sales personnel. On-line retail businesses require only a warehouse for storage and shipping. As a result, such businesses should experience significant savings in operating costs because rent and payroll account for more than 80 percent of a retail business' fixed, or operating, expenses.

CONCLUSION: The retail method markup of 52 percent is equal to the cost method markup of 1.0833.

EXERCISES

REMINDER: When using the cost method of markup to determine the retail price, always add "1" to the cost percentage and multiply by the cost.

Example: Cost = $100

MU = 150%

MU 150% = Cost $100 × 2.5 = $250 Retail

Find the markup percentages for the following using the cost method of inventory.

1. Retail = $10

Cost = $4

2. Retail = $620

Cost = $300

3. Retail = $18

    Cost = $9.50

4. Retail = $42,000

    Cost = $23,230

Find the markup percentages for the following using the retail method of inventory.

5. Retail = $6.00

    Cost = $2.50

6. Retail = $88

    Cost = $39

7. Retail = $3,500

    Cost = $1,685

8. Retail = $62,500

    Cost = $30,500

Convert the following cost markups to their retail markup equivalents:

9.   1.75

10. 1.20

11. 1.95

12. 1.50

Convert the following retail markups to their cost markup equivalents:

13. 48%

14. 50%

15. 52.5%

16. 54%

PROJECT

Explain how a major retail outlet would negotiate a sale with a European manufacturer. Include the correct markup conversion, the impact of international sales on-line, and turn.

PART TWO
Analyzing Financial Documents

Anyone interested in the growth of a public company—from stockholders, potential stockholders, and financial analysts to employees, vendors, and consumers—should stay informed about its financial status. One of the best ways to achieve this goal is to examine a company's financial records. Fortunately, all corporations that issue common stock publicly must submit a yearly financial statement that becomes part of the public record. These reports are included in the company's annual report, or 10K.

In Part Two, Chapters 8 and 9 explain how to interpret two parts of a company's financial statement—the profit-and-loss statement, also known as the income or operating statement, and the balance sheet. Many individuals ignore these documents, as well as stock market reports, because they are unfamiliar with many of the technical terms. Once these terms are understood, however, the individual should feel comfortable and confident in negotiating the world of finance.

In analyzing income statements, keep in mind that retail business is one of the nation's leading economic indicators, along with housing statistics, the unemployment rate, the gross national product, the stock market, and interest rates. Evaluating the profits or losses in any of these indicators helps to better understand the country's economic status.

Retail sales are important in measuring the "confidence level" of consumers. The general assumption is that consumers engage in more impulse buying when their perception is that the economy is strong. When consumers lose confidence in the economy, they will hold on to their funds and defer discretionary purchases. Thus, a quarterly increase in retail sales usually means an increase in consumer confidence.

One of the most frequently asked questions about businesses has always been, "How do you really know if a company's financial statement is accurate?" In light of recent developments, that question has acquired new importance. The United States is confronted with accounting scandals, examples of corporate malfeasance, stock market instability, and the declining value of mutual funds that are profoundly impacting consumer and investor confidence. Even companies reporting good **earnings** are suffering from the public's growing distrust of corporate financial statements. So, how indeed does one judge the accuracy of a corporation's financial statement? The final two chapters are devoted to creating light in the gray areas of financial statements.

CHAPTER 8 / Profit-and-Loss Statements

The **profit-and-loss (P/L) statement,** which is also called an operating statement or an income statement, lists a business' total revenues (sales) and total expenses (costs). The difference between revenues and expenses is the profit or loss.

COMPONENTS OF THE P/L STATEMENT

The first component of a P/L statement is net sales, which is obtained by subtracting returns and allowances from **gross** (or total) **sales.** The second component is gross margin (or gross profit), which is determined by subtracting the cost of goods sold from net sales. The cost of goods sold is simply the total cost in materials and labor of the products sold. Gross margin is the focus of this text, as it is gross margin that determines profits.

EVALUATING THE P/L STATEMENT

Gross margin dollars are used to pay all operating expenses. If a company's gross margin exceeds its operating expenses, the company can claim profits. If, however, operating expenses exceed gross margin, the company shows a loss.

As seen in the following example, the same amount of total sales can produce different results depending on operating expenses.

Net sales	$200,000		Net sales	$200,000
− Cost of goods sold	− $120,000		− Cost of goods sold	− $120,000
Gross margin	$ 80,000		Gross margin	$ 80,000
− Operating expenses	− $ 75,000		− Operating expenses	− $ 85,000
Profit	+ $ 5,000		Loss	− $ 5,000

CASH FLOW

More companies go out of business due to poor cash flow than due to lack of profit. Your business must be "liquid": able to meet short-term debt. For example, examine this P/L statement:

Net sales		$800,000
− CMS		450,000
Gross margin		350,000
− Operating expense		320,000
Profit	+	30,000

Even though a profit exists, it may not exist in a liquid or usable form. For example, if that profit is tied up in unsold inventory you cannot sell, then you cannot use that money to pay bills.

In retail mathematics, it is often true that the percentages of each component of a P/L statement are more important than the actual dollar amounts. The reason is that not all retail businesses are the same size. Therefore, comparisons of dollar amounts may not be fair. Percentages, however, can be compared usefully.

For example, look at the P/L statements below for two shoe companies. ABC Shoes has 20 stores; XYZ has only one store.

	ABC Shoes	**XYZ Shoes**
Net sales	10,000,000	1,000,000
− Cost of goods sold	− 6,000,000	− 600,000
Gross margin	4,000,000	400,000
− Operating expenses	− 3,800,000	− 300,000
P/L	+ 200,000	+ 100,000
	Net profit 2%	Net profit 10%

The profit dollars for ABC are double that of XYZ, yet XYZ is being run with greater efficiency and profitability.

In evaluating a P/L statement, however, another factor has to be included in the determination of profitability. After computing profitability based on gross margin dollars, the corporation has to pay interest to bondholders. (**Bonds** are sold to finance company debt.) Once this interest is deducted, the corporation can determine its pretax profit.

For example,

Net sales	$10,000,000
− Cost of goods sold	− $ 6,000,000
Gross margin	$ 4,000,000
− Operating expenses	− $ 3,500,000
Profit	$ 500,000
− Interest due bondholders	− $ 100,000
Pretax profits	$ 400,000

In this example, after paying bondholders $100,000 interest, the pretax profit is $400,000. From this pretax profit, the corporation now

INSIDE SCOOP

The Rise and Fall of Corporate Confidence

In the year 2002, the economy was in a state of "repression," which is a combination of recession and depression. This was compounded by the collapse of a number of corporate giants amid charges of misstated earnings, overvalued assets, accounting malfeasance, and unethical behavior.

Among the giants to fall, WorldCom filed the largest-ever bankruptcy case as a result of financial mismanagement in July 2002. The greatest attention, however, was focused on the Enron Corporation, which filed bankruptcy even though its sales exceeded one billion dollars. In managing Enron's financial records, Arthur Andersen, one of the best-known accounting firms in the United States, was accused of such improprieties as exaggerating earnings, causing a false sense of security and optimism among investors.

One of the most complicated types of misstated earnings involved the issuing of stock options to employees. By giving options that are due for payment sometime in the future, companies were able to avoid reporting these debts as liabilities.

Vivid news coverage of these events, often involving millionaire corporate executives and high-profile personalities, added to the public's loss of confidence in the stock market and further weakened the economy. The government and the Securities and Exchange Commission have taken and continue to take steps to prevent such improprieties in the future.

subtracts all corporate taxes, which range from 30 percent to 45 percent. With a 35 percent tax rate, the above P/L statement now shows the following:

Net sales	$10,000,000
− Cost of goods sold	−$ 6,000,000
Gross margin	$ 4,000,000
− Operating expenses	−$ 3,500,000
Profit	$ 500,000
− Interest due bondholders	−$ 100,000
Pretax profits	$ 400,000
− Taxes (35%)	−$ 140,000
Profit	$ 260,000

To determine net profits, the corporation now has to deduct all **dividends** that must be paid to common or preferred stockholders. (**Stock** in this context is shares of ownership in a corporation.) Keep in mind that the Board of Directors decides whether common stockholders will receive dividends.

EXERCISES

For one through four, complete each of the following skeletal income statements. The expressions cost of merchandise sold and cost of goods sold are interchangeable.

1.
Net sales	$350,000
− CMS	_____
GM	$150,000
− OPX	_____
P/L	⟨− $ 10,000⟩

2.
Net sales	$618,000
− CMS	_____
GM	40%
− OPX	_____
P/L	+ 5%

3.

Net sales	$415,000	
− CMS	_____	
GM		
− OPX	45%	
P/L	− 3%	

4.

Net sales		
− CMS	_____	
GM	45%	
− OPX	_____	
P/L	$20,000 + 10%	

5. A business gave the following facts concerning its yearly income statement: "For 2001, we had a cost of merchandise sold of 58 percent and operating expenses of 44 percent."

    a.   Did this business have a profit or loss for 2002?

    b.   What was the percentage of that profit or loss?

For questions six through eight, find the net earnings (profits) for the given situations.

6. Company DEF had the following income statement for the year 2001. It also paid $60,000 interest on bonds and had corporate taxes of 35 percent.

$$\text{Net sales} = \$1,300,000$$
$$\text{CMS} = \$\ 700,000$$
$$\text{GM} = \$\ 600,000$$
$$\text{OPX} = \$\ 400,000$$
$$\text{P/L} =$$
$$\text{Net earnings}$$

7.   Company GHI had the following income statement:

$$\text{Net sales} = \$17,000,000$$

$$\text{CMS} = \$10,000,000$$

$$\text{GM} = \$\ 7,000,000$$

$$\text{OPX} = \$\ 5,500,000$$

$$\text{P/L} = \$\ 1,500,000$$

In addition, it paid 40 percent corporate tax. Find the net earnings.

8.   Company JKL showed the following income statement:

$$\text{Net sales} = \$60,000,000$$

$$\text{CMS} = \$35,000,000$$

$$\text{GM} = \$25,000,000$$

$$\text{OPX} = \$24,000,000$$

$$\text{P/L} =$$

In addition, this company paid taxes at a 35 percent rate, interest of $300,000, and dividends of $200,000. Find the net income.

9. A business with a gross margin of 38 percent had a 2 percent loss. What were the operating expenses expressed as a percentage?

10. A company had a gross margin of 41 percent and operating expenses of 41 percent. What was the profit or loss?

11. A company had a profit of 5 percent, with operating expenses of 42 percent. What was the gross margin percentage?

12. A business had a cost of merchandise sold of 60 percent, with a 4 percent loss in profit. What were the operating expenses expressed as a percentage?

13. A business had a 5 percent profit and operating expenses of 40 percent. What was the cost of merchandise expressed as a percentage?

PROJECT

A company is considering whether to issue bonds or preferred stock to raise capital. In either case, the company would pay the same interest or dividends rate for the amount borrowed. One of the company's executives said, "If we issue bonds it would leave us with a higher profit margin." Question: Is that statement true or false? Explain your reasoning.

CHAPTER 9 / Balance Sheets

A corporation has two additional documents that can be used to analyze its profitability: the balance sheet and the cash flow chart. The most basic element of a balance sheet is its ability to weigh, or balance, its components. In a basic balance sheet, a firm's total assets should always equal the sum of its liabilities plus stockholders **equity**, as shown below.

Current assets

Cash	$ 600,000
Accounts receivable	$ 300,000
+ Inventory	$ 850,000
Total current assets	$1,750,000
+ Building long term	$1,200,000
Total assets	$2,950,000

Current liabilities

Accounts payable	$ 500,000
+ Accrued expenses	$ 320,000
Total current liabilities	$ 820,000
+ Notes and loans	$ 260,000
Total liabilities	$1,080,000
+ Stockholders equity	$1,870,000
Total liabilities and stockholders equity:	$2,950,000

A firm's balance sheet that is out of balance indicates a financial shortage of funds. These funds must be raised by outside means, that is, bonds, stocks, or loans.

A balance sheet is a gold mine of financial information. It helps in answering the following questions:

Is this business profitable?

Is the value of the business increasing?

Is stock turning over fast enough?

What is the worth of the business?

A balance sheet is mandatory to:

establish credit

apply for loans

file income tax returns

Finally, a balance sheet is used to determine whether a corporation's capital investment was sound.

It is essential to understand every component of the balance sheet. Of equal importance is understanding the implications and tacit nuances of this financial instrument. For example, an extremely profitable business may have little or no net worth. In contrast, a business may have a huge net worth, but be unable to pay its operating expenses.

BALANCE SHEET BASICS

A business is always in a condition of equality. What it owns equals what it owes, either to its creditors or to its owners. This is represented by the formula:

$$\text{Assets} = \text{Liabilities} + \text{Owners' equity}$$

The owners' equity is what the business owes the owners.

To understand this basic premise, suppose a novelty toy business opens with $50,000 opening capital. According to the formula, assets = liabilities + owners equity:

$$\text{Cash } \$50,000 = 0 + \$50,000$$

This simple balance sheet is in a state of equality. Now suppose the buyer takes $10,000 cash to buy toys at wholesale to sell. The balance sheet now looks like this:

$$\text{Assets} = \text{Liabilities} + \text{Owners equity}$$
$$\text{Cash } \$40,000 = 0 + \$40,000$$
$$\text{Toy inventory } \$10,000 = 0 + \$10,000$$

Remember that in the U.S. form of capitalism, the owners of the business (stockholders) own the entire equity. In this example, the balance sheet is in balance:

Assets

Cash	40,000	= 0 + 40,000
Inventory	10,000	= 0 + 10,000
	$50,000	= 0 + $50,000

Examination of a corporation's assets and liabilities involves all the following factors:

Current Assets	= **Cash on hand**
	Marketable securities
	Inventory
	Accounts receivable
	Goodwill
Long-term assets	= Buildings/land
	Equipment
Liabilities (current)	= Notes and loans
	Accrued expenses
	Accounts payable
Liabilities (long-term)	= Long-term notes
	Mortgages
	Bonds payable

WHAT IS A BUSINESS WORTH?

The simple answer to this question is: "whatever the market will pay for it." However, to fairly determine the value of a business, the most widely accepted formula is the Net Worth Ratio formula:

Net worth = Total assets − Total liabilities

After computing this ratio, "goodwill," which is difficult to put a monetary value on, needs to be added.

BALANCE SHEET COMPONENTS

In addition to defining the components, this section will also examine the risk attached to the misuse (intentional or unintentional) of information about each component.

What Are Assets?

Assets are anything a business owns that has monetary value. In evaluating assets, one must keep an open mind about the risks of relying too much on a firm's financial statement. The most accurate assets are usually the long-term assets. Buildings and land, for example, usually increase in value over time, so inflated estimates of their worth may prove less risky than with current assets.

Some controls do exist over a business' declaration of its assets. If a business intentionally overstates the value of an asset, a felony charge may be pursued. In addition, the Securities and Exchange Commission (SEC) may halt the trading of the business' stock. Among the most important assets of a business are marketable securities, inventory, **accounts receivable**, goodwill, and, of course, cash.

MARKETABLE SECURITIES

Marketable securities include any securities, stocks, bonds, options, and mutual funds owned by the business. In analyzing a balance sheet, remember that a successful company has a balanced portfolio that includes a variety of these investment options, which are valued at 70 percent of their current market value.

An uninformed purchaser can easily underestimate the impact of a change in marketable securities assets. For example, investors purchase a business that lists marketable securities of a certain value, but all of these securities are in one high-tech firm. Overnight, the high-tech firm experiences a devastating event that results in a 50 percent drop in its value. The purchasers now own a firm worth much less than anticipated.

INVENTORY

Inventory consists of any products that a company sells as either finished products or as raw components. Assessing the value of inventory is the single greatest challenge in determining the true value of a company. The main reason is that inventory is valued at its cost to the business, but that cost may not represent its value. For example, a buyer purchases 10,000 dresses at $10 cost per dress. Although this inventory is now valued at $100,000, that value is only accurate if there is a market for the product. If the dresses were made in an ugly burlap fabric that no one wants, what is the intrinsic value of the inventory? Only the consumer can decide this. So although the books will show a value or asset of inventory for $100,000, the real worth may be zero. Therefore, whenever the asset value for inventory is examined, one must look at its current market value. Imagine an investor's dismay at discovering that the assets of a recently acquired business were totally inflated and that the actual net worth of the business had to be deflated or adjusted to determine a true net worth of considerably less value.

ACCOUNTS RECEIVABLE

Accounts receivable represents all the money owed to a company for products and services. Once again, this asset is easy prey for either intentional or unintentional miscalculations. Why? Because no matter what value a business places in its annual report for accounts receivable, there is no certainty that the business will collect its receivables.

Here is a short list of common reasons why a business does not collect all its receivables:

1. The debtor is deceased. Try collecting from the estate! It is practically impossible.
2. The debtor disputes the debt by claiming some defect or problem with the product that will now require resolution by a court.
3. The debtor files bankruptcy. Now the business will, if lucky, collect a small portion of the debt. Generally, a business loses all funds due to it when a firm or individual is granted bankruptcy protection.

So once again a company's assets may be highly inflated.

GOODWILL

Goodwill consists of all intangibles a firm may have. For instance, a firm may have a desirable designer name that it can license to other ancillary companies. In this instance, goodwill is a perfect example of pure market interest because any value may be placed on a licensing fee. Its fair value is determined by whatever a person or business will pay for it in the open market.

What Are Liabilities?

Liabilities are any real debt accrued by a business. In evaluating a firm's liabilities, the key factor is to make certain that all liabilities are stated. Often, toward the end of an accounting period, all actual debt is not shown. Just as with overstating the value of one's assets, understating the value of one's liabilities, that is, hiding debt, is a felony. Liabilities include accounts payable, accrued expenses, and notes and loans. Accounts payable are legal debts that a company is obligated to pay. **Accrued expenses** are operational expenses that accrue for a short period of time before payment is made. **Notes and loans** are debts—both short-term and long-term (longer than one year)—that the company pays off in a monthly payment of interest and principal.

RATIO ANALYSIS OF FINANCIAL STATEMENTS

An important aspect of retail profitability is the ability to apply quantitative analysis to a company's financial statement.

Liquidity Ratios

Liquidity is the ability of a business to meet its short-term debt or liabilities. Remember that more companies go out of business because of a lack of cash flow than because of a lack of profits. If a business has its assets tied up in inventory and receivables, and if sales are slow or receivables are slow in being collected, the business will not have enough cash on hand to pay its bills.

Two key formulas are used to evaluate a company's liquidity. The first formula is called the "current ratio":

$$\text{Current ratio} = \frac{\text{Current assets}}{\text{Current liabilities}}$$

Once the calculation is completed, a company's liquidity can be judged by "rating the ratio solution." For the current ratio:

2+	= Excellent liquidity
1.5–2	= Good liquidity
1.25–1.49	= Fair liquidity
1.0–1.24	= Poor liquidity
less than 1	= Severe lack of liquidity

The second formula is the "quick ratio," which deletes inventory from the formula because the value of inventory, as discussed above, is often difficult to accurately assess:

$$\text{Quick Ratio} = \frac{\text{Current assets} - \text{Inventory}}{\text{Current liabilities}}$$

When using this formula, the answer must be evaluated against the following ratings:

1.0+	= Excellent
.8–.9	= Good
.6–.7	= Fair
less than .6	= Poor

To apply these formulas, look at the following charts for Company ABC in the year 2001.

Company ABC Income Statement (in millions)	2001	2000
Net Sales	$80.0	$102.0
Cost of Goods Sold	50.0	60.0
Gross Profit	30.0	42.0
Operating Expenses	25.0	38.0
Pre-tax income	5.0	4.0
Income taxes at 35%	1.75	1.4
Net Income	3.25	2.6

Balance Sheet (in millions)	2001	2000
Assets: Current Cash	$ 3.0	$ 4.5
Accounts Receivable	2.0	2.5
Inventory	5.0	7.0
Total Current Assets	10.0	14.0
Long-term assets plant	6.0	6.0
Total Assets	16.0	20.0
Liabilities: Current	3.0	4.5
Long-term	8.5	10.5
Total Liabilities	11.5	15.5
Stockholders Equity Common Stock:	4.5	4.5
450,000, par value $10		
Total Stockholders Equity	4.5	4.5
Total Liabilities and Stockholders Equity	16.0	20.0

First, apply the current ratio formula, as follows:

$$\text{Current Ratio} = \frac{\text{Current assets}}{\text{Current liabilities}}$$

$$\text{Company ABC} = \frac{10.0}{3.0} = 3.3$$

In this example of the ABC Corporation, the liquidity rate of 3.3 is excellent liquidity.

Next, use the same information to measure liquidity by the quick ratio:

$$\text{Quick Ratio} = \frac{\text{Current assets} - \text{Inventory}}{\text{Current liabilities}}$$

$$\text{Company ABC} = 5/3 = 1.66$$

Note that ABC's liquidity rating is also excellent with this formula.

Leverage Ratios

These three ratios, also known as solvency ratios, measure the possible negative effect of excessive debt, as well as the soundness of a company's finances.

NET WORTH FORMULA

This extremely important ratio tells the current book value of the business. It is expressed as follows:

$$\text{Net worth} = \text{Total assets} - \text{Total liabilities}$$

There is no ratings guide for net worth, as it is a purely suggestive number. For instance, if a business began with $50,000 and had a net worth of $100,000 at the end of its first year, that would be excellent. However, if a business was started with a net worth of $1,000,000 and was worth $400,000 after one year, the loss of net worth would be substantial. Remember that net worth is equal to equity.

For Company ABC, the formula would yield:

$$\begin{array}{r} 16.0 \\ -\ 11.5 \\ \hline =\ \ 4.5 \end{array}$$

CURRENT LIABILITIES TO NET WORTH

This formula computes the money due to creditors within the next 12 months as a percentage of the stockholders' net worth. If liabilities increase compared to net worth, creditors are less secure about receiving timely payment. The ratio is determined by the following formula:

$$\frac{\text{Current liabilities}}{\text{Net worth}}$$

The results are rated as follows:

50%–60% = Excellent creditor security

61%–70% = Good creditor security

71%–79% = Fair creditor security

80%+   = Very poor creditor security

If this is applied to the ABC Company in the previous example, the result is:

$$\text{Company ABC} = \frac{3.0}{4.5} = 67\%$$

Thus, the ABC Company shows strong **solvency** as the net worth far exceeds the current debt.

DEBT RATIO

This ratio determines the percentage of a company's assets that is pledged to creditors. The formula is:

$$\text{Debt ratio} = \frac{\text{Total liabilities}}{\text{Total assets}}$$

The ratio is then evaluated as follows:

75%   = Poor solvency

65%–74% = Fair solvency

60%–64% = Good solvency

under 59% = Excellent solvency

Apply the formula to the ABC Company in the previous example:

$$\frac{11.5}{16.0} = 72\%$$

Thus the ABC Company's solvency rating is "fair."

PROFITABILITY FORMULAS

These calculations examine profit based on a number of different factors.

Profitability Margin

The profitability margin is determined by the following formula:

$$\text{Profit margin} = \frac{\text{Net income}}{\text{Net sales}} \text{(profit)}$$

Remember that profit can be shown as either pretax or posttax with dividends. Always make certain that the profit used in the above formula is the net profit after taxes and dividends. The resulting profit percentage is then evaluated according to the following:

Loss   = No dividends to offer shareholders
1%–3%   = Poor
4%–7%   = Fair
8%–10% = Good
10%+   = Excellent

Again, using the ABC Company, apply the formula:

$$\text{Company ABC} = \frac{\$3.25 \text{ (in millions)}}{\$80 \text{ (in millions)}} = 4\%$$

This company has a "fair" rating.

Gross Profit Margin (Gross Margin)

Gross profit margin is the single most important factor in determining the profitability of any retail business. To determine GPM, use the following formula:

$$\text{Gross profit margin} = \frac{\text{Gross profit}}{\text{Net sales}}$$

The resulting percentage should be evaluated according to the following:

45%+	= Excellent
40%–44%	= Good
35%–39%	= Fair
30%–34%	= Poor
less than 30%	= Extremely poor

NOTE: The above ratings are only for retail businesses. If a manufacturer also has retail outlets, the gross profit margin ratings are different from the above. For manufacturers and manufacturers that have retail outlets, the percentage should be evaluated as follows:

35%+	= Excellent
30%–34%	= Good
25%–29%	= Fair
under 25%	= Poor

For the ABC Company, which is a retail business, the formula yields:

$$\text{ABC Company} = \frac{\$30.0 \ (\text{in millions})}{80.0 \ (\text{in millions})} = 37.5\%$$

Thus, the ABC Company has a "fair" rating.

Return on Total Assets

This ratio examines how a company uses its total assets and how it is converting its assets into profits. The formula is:

$$\text{Return on total assets} = \frac{\text{Net income}}{\text{Total assets}}$$

The resulting percentage is evaluated as follows:

$$20\%+ \quad = \text{Excellent}$$
$$15\%–19\% = \text{Very good}$$
$$10\%–14\% = \text{Good}$$
$$5\%–9\% \quad = \text{Fair}$$
$$\text{under } 5\% = \text{Poor}$$

Again, apply the formula to the ABC Company as follows:

$$\text{ABC Company} = \frac{\$3.25 \text{ (in millions)}}{16.0 \text{ (in millions)}} = 20\%$$

The ABC Company has an "excellent" rating.

STOCK MARKET VALUE FORMULAS

Book Value Per Share

This ratio states the actual value of the company's stock, but not on the open market. This means that the book value of a company is not influenced by the market's supply and demand dynamics. To determine the book value per share, use the following formula:

$$\text{Book value per share} = \frac{\text{Stockholder's equity}}{\text{Common stock outstanding}}$$

The ABC Company has 450,000 shares of outstanding common stock. If this formula is applied to the ABC Company, it yields:

$$\text{ABC Company} = \frac{\$4.5 \text{ (in millions)}}{.450 \text{ (in millions)}} = \$10$$

The book value per share of ABC's common stock is $10. To understand what this means, the book value per share must be compared to the current market value of the company.

INSIDE SCOOP

Understanding Stock Market Listings

Once you have gained insight regarding a company's financial data and its strengths and weaknesses, the stock market ratios should help you determine whether financial statements support the current market value of a stock. To interpret the stock market listings, however, it is necessary to understand the basic rules governing the computations used to calculate stock market quotations.

Following is an example of a listing that might appear in your local newspaper. Explanations of the columns follow the chart.

Hi-Low	Stock	Sym	Ref	Divid	Yield	PE	Volume	Hi-Low	Close	Change
52–14	ABC	A	A	.60	1.6	16	100	39.37	38.25	+ .62
8–2	DEF	D	B	.00	0	21	87	7.5–7.25	7.25	− .13
74–49	GHI	G	P	.84	1.7	4	301	50.37–50.14	50.25	+ 2.38
36–29	JKL	J	A	1.21	3.8	48	1004	32–31	31.50	
18–23	MNO	M	A	.24	*	20	395	22–20	*	− .37
41–30	PQR	P	P	.30	1.0	16	87	33–32.5	30.13	
63–22	STU	S	B	.80	*	54	736	62.20–57	*	+ 1.87
6–5	VWX	V	P	.00	—	71	450	5.25–5.87	5.75	

HI-LOW (FIRST HI-LOW)

This column shows the high and low points of the stock over a 52-week period. This is an important indicator because it reflects a stock's "volatility." A stock is said to be "stable" when there is less than a 15 percent change from its low and its high selling price during this period. For example, if a certain stock's Hi-Low was 10–3, it means that the stock sold as high as $10 per share and as low as $3 per share.

If you purchased this stock at the high point, $10 per share, and its current market value is $3 per share, that represents a substantial loss of 70 percent. Thus, that stock would be considered very volatile.

Now, look at another stock. Its Hi-Low was 82–69. If you purchased this stock at the high price of $82 per share, and its current market value is $69 per share, your loss is only 16 percent. This is a borderline stable stock.

Remember it is not the dollar difference between the high and low price that determines volatility, but rather the percentage difference. For example, the stock whose Hi-Low was 10–3 has a difference of $7, while the stock with the Hi-Low of 82–69 has a difference of $13. Even though the latter stock had a larger dollar loss, it is still much more stable, or safe.

Evaluating a yearly Hi-Low is also an important consideration when deciding whether to buy a particular stock at the current market value. For example, you are considering purchasing stock DEF at a current market value of $7.25 per share. Examining the current stock quotation, you discover the 52-week Hi-Low is 8–2. You would correctly conclude, "Why should I buy this stock now, when in the past year it has reached a high of $8 and has such volatility that it has been as low as $2?" It would be unwise to purchase this stock so near its high.

In general, it is poor strategy to buy a stock at its 52-week high because logic dictates that it will drop again in price. If you choose to buy at a 52-week high, it is known as "chasing the high."

STOCK

This column names the specific stock.

SYM

This symbol lists the company name in shorthand.

REF

Often stocks are followed by a letter or series of letters, of which the most common are A and B. These letters designate whether the particular stock pays dividends or offers voting rights. P means "preferred stock."

DIVID

The dividend lists how much monetary dividend the stock pays.

YIELD

Yield tells what percentage the dividend is paying per share. Before yield can be calculated, you need to find the current market closing price value. Then, divide the dividend by the closing market price to determine the yield percentage. For example, stock ABC pays a $0.60 dividend. Its closing price for the day was $38.25. Therefore,

$$\text{Yield} = \frac{\text{Dividend}}{\text{Closing price}} = \frac{\$0.60}{38.25} = 1.6\%$$

Stock ABC's yield is 1.6 percent.

PE (PRICE-EARNINGS MULTIPLE)

PE has already been discussed. To calculate the PE, one needs to know the EPS (earnings per share).

VOLUME

The volume column provides the number of shares traded in the thousands.

HI-LOW (SECOND HI-LOW)

This column shows the Hi-Low trading range for that specific day.

CLOSE

This column gives the final trading price of the day's session.

CHANGE

This column shows the change in the stock's value from one day to the next.

Current Stock Market Valuation

To ascertain the current market price of a company, two facts are needed: the book value, as determined above, and the market value, as determined by the current price of a share on the market. For this example, ABC Company has a closing price on the New York Stock Exchange of $20 per share. So now, ABC Company has the following two values:

Book value: $10 per share

Market value: $20 per share

A comparison of the values makes it clear that the current market has confidence in the company and is willing to pay a market value that exceeds the book value of ABC stock. In other words, the market value of a company's stock is a "confidence meter." If a company's market value exceeds the book value, then one deduces that the "market" has confidence in the company. If, on the other hand, a company's book value exceeds the market value, then there are two possible explanations. One is negative, while the other is positive. The explanations are:

1. The market has no confidence in the company.
2. The market has not yet fully valued the stock. If so, this might be an excellent underpriced stock to purchase.

So how does one decide what to do when one interpretation of an indicator says, "buy this stock," and a second implies the reverse. Professional security dealers can be found who will support both arguments. The individual interested in purchasing stock should evaluate the company's history, current success, and the strength of its financial statements, and then decide for oneself. Since its founding in 1792, the market has proven only one thing—its unpredictability.

Earnings Per Share

This formula is the most illuminating of them all. The ratio indicates how much money stockholders will receive in the event of the company's bankruptcy. The market value has no influence in determining the actual payback value. Earnings per share is determined by using the following formula:

$$\text{Earnings per share} = \frac{\text{Net income (profit)}}{\text{Common stock outstanding}}$$

If applied to ABC Company, it yields:

$$\text{ABC Company} = \frac{\$3,250,000}{450,000} = \$7.22$$

Thus, earnings per share for the ABC Company is $7.22.

The question then remains, "Do stockholders get anything in the event of bankruptcy?" The answer usually is "yes." The stockholders are entitled to the earnings per share value, but that value is further diminished by attorneys' fees, interests, and assets not collected. In ABC Company's bankruptcy, the individual shareholder will receive only a portion of the $7.22 per share. Sometimes, litigation and inflated assets will leave nothing for its stockholders.

THE DOW

The Dow Jones is a group of 65 companies in the areas of commerce, transportation, and utilities that is used as a weather vane for the performance of the stock market in general. Many traders live or die by interpreting the "Dow's indications."

Many books have been written about the Dow. Some argue the merits of the information gleaned from the Dow; others dispute the reliability of the Dow as a source of information.

In evaluating the stock market, consider the "Random Walk Theory": no one really knows for sure what will happen.

Price/Earnings Ratio

Commonly called PE Ratio, this formula is valuable for evaluating a company's intrinsic value compared to the current market value of its stock. Thus,

$$\text{Price/earnings ratio} = \frac{\text{Current market value}}{\text{Earnings per share}}$$

If applied to the ABC Company, it yields:

$$\text{ABC Company} = \frac{\$20}{7.22} = 2.8$$

Understanding the Price/Earnings Multiple

The percentage finding from the above ratio needs to be evaluated against the following table:

1–15	The stock is not fully valued, and should therefore obtain substantial growth.
16–39	The current market price is properly valued.
40–60	The current market price is slightly overvalued.
61–79	The current market price is overvalued.
80–100	The current market price is very overvalued.
100+	This is a severely overpriced stock.

Thus, the ABC Company's PE Ratio of 2.8 means that the company's stock is selling for almost three times its actual earnings. Because this is a low number, it usually means that the stock market is undervaluing the stock at its current price of $20 per share and that the stock has plenty of room for growth (meaning that the market price can rise quite a bit and that the stock remains a good value).

Because this is such an important ratio, other examples need to be studied. In the highly profitable, high-tech era of the late 1990s, most high-tech companies were so severely overpriced that the bubble eventually had to burst, and when it did large companies lost millions and small investors found their investments diminished.

OVER-THE-COUNTER TABLES: DEFINITIONS OF ABBREVIATIONS

The abbreviations, defined below, need to be understood in order to interpret the stock market tables.

A	Class A issue
B	Class B issue
C	Stock exempt from NASDAQ listing specifications for a limited period
D	New issue
E	Company is delinquent in filing data with the Securities and Exchange Commission (SEC)
F	Foreign issue
G	Convertible bond, 1st issue
H, I	Convertible bond issue, 2nd and 3rd issues
J	Voting issue
K	Nonvoting issue
L	Issue does not carry all rights
M,N,O	Various issues of preferred stock
P	Preferred stock, first issue
Q	Company in bankruptcy
R	Preemptive rights
T	Includes warrants
U	Combination package of securities
V	Issue to be released later
WI	Issue to be released later
Y	Issue in an American depository receipt

For example, the AJAX Company, which developed software, had earnings per share of $0.10, but the current market price was $100.00 per share. As a result, the PE ratio was:

$$\text{PE ratio} = \frac{\$100}{0.10} = 1,000$$

This means that the AJAX Company's stock was selling at 1,000 times its true value. When high-tech companies began to suffer losses in 1999 and stocks declined, the PE ratios started to more accurately reflect the true financial statuses of the companies. Unfortunately, the true statuses were so much lower that losses were severe.

INTERPRETING DATA

Based on our study of the ABC Company, what questions should be asked and what conclusions can be drawn?

Two questions are asked to determine the current financial status of a company. The first requires a comparison between the company's current financial statement and last year's statement to determine what is called the "analysis of trend." Such a comparison of a company's financial statements from one year to another can help determine whether the company is heading in a profitable or unprofitable direction. After the trend analysis is completed, a company's finances can be more accurately compared to the overall standard of performance in the industry.

The strengths and weaknesses of a company become more apparent when the areas of liquidity, leverage, profitability, and stock market formulas are examined. In reviewing a company's financial statement, always verify the data before placing confidence in its evaluations by determining:

whether inventory value is true in "Today's Market Standing"

whether receivables are collectible

whether all liabilities are included

the components of operating expenses

the value of goodwill

that all expenses have been tallied

whether the corporate charter contains any deleterious clauses

---

INSIDE SCOOP

Roller Coaster Ride

After the boom years of 1988 to 1998, many investors are asking, "What has happened to the economy, the stock market, and consumer confidence?" Among the many possible answers are the consequences of the terrorist attacks on September 11, 2001, the war with Iraq, and a general lack of confidence in current leadership. Then again, perhaps none of those factors has anything to do with today's climate. The fact may be that nothing is really wrong with the present economy. The proper question may be, "What caused the incredible and artificial boom from 1988 to 1998?"

The economy during that decade was characterized by soaring stocks in high-technology companies that produced no actual product. These companies often traded on the Nasdaq at price-earnings ratios of 10,000 to 1. Thus, during the 10-year period from 1988 to 1998, investors seemed to have abandoned all previous market indicators to take advantage of the boom in high-technology companies. People were seduced by seemingly unlimited earnings, and investors turned away from proven blue-chip stocks. That decade was the unusual time, the aberration.

As the Dow Jones leaped from 1,750 to 12,000, investors and analysts should have asked, "What is wrong?" But investors were seduced by high profits, and few people listened to more sober analysts.

Then, in March of 1998, Alan Greenspan, Chairman of the Federal Reserve Board, announced that things were "too good." Many analysts believe that these words kindled the fire that began the downward spiral that continued into the twenty-first century. But, whatever the cause, the market bottomed out and returned to more realistic levels. High-technology businesses that had ludicrously inflated price-earnings ratios now were brought into line. Today's economy is more in balance with previous increases.

The only explanation for this roller coaster ride is confidence. The economy and the stock markets worldwide reflect consumer and business confidence.

EXERCISES

1. Using the financial ratio grids and the charts for the ABC Company on page 148, perform the following analyses for the year 2000:

    a. Calculate all ratios for the ABC Company in 2000. For this calculation, note that the current stock market value is $18 per share.

    b. Compare each ratio to the year 2001 calculation and determine if the company's financial status has improved or deteriorated compared to the previous year.

2. Using the financial grid ratios and the charts for the XYZ Company for the year 2001, answer the following questions. Note that the company's stock closed at $29 per share on the stock exchange. Compute the following ratio problems for the fiscal year 2001. In addition, relate the analysis of XYZ Company to the industry average where applicable.

   a.   Current ratio

   b.   Quick ratio

   c.   Current liabilities to net worth

   d.   Net worth

   e.   Debt ratio

   f.   Profit margin

   g.   Gross profit margin

   h.   Return on total assets

   i.   Book value

   j.   Earnings per share

   k.   PE multiple

Company XYZ Income Statement in Millions	2001
Net Sales	$90.0
Cost of Goods Sold	55.0
Gross Profit	35.0
Operating Expenses	29.0
Pre-tax Profit	6.0
Taxes at 35%	2.1
Net Income	3.9

Balance Sheet	2001
Assets: Current Cash	3.3
Accounts Receivable	2.3
Inventory	6.1
Total Current Assets	11.7
Long-term Assets Plan	5.0
Total Assets	16.7
Liabilities: Current	3.8
Long-term	5.7
Total Liabilities	9.5
Stockholders Equity Common Stock	7.2
66,000 Shares at 12 Par Value	
Total Stockholders Equity	7.2
Total Liabilities and Stockholders Equity	16.7

Questions 3 through 11 are based on the stock market chart in the box entitled "Understanding Stock Market Listings."

3. Would you consider ABC stock to be highly volatile? Why?

4. What was ABC Stock's closing price as of yesterday?

5. Considering only companies DEF and GHI, which company's stock is less volatile and why?

6. If JKL's closing price yesterday was $32.38, find the net change.

7. If MNO closed yesterday at $19.25, find today's closing price.

8. If PQR's closing price yesterday was $28.63, find the net change.

9. If STU closed yesterday at $59.50, find today's closing price.

10. If VWX's closing price yesterday was $4.83, find the net change.

11. Calculate the yield for the following stocks:
    a. GHI
    b. MNO
    c. STU

Questions 12 through 17 are based on the following stock table:

52 Week Hi	Low	Stock	Div	Yld%	P/E	Sales 100s	Last	Net Chg
35.50	20.50	LNR Prop **LNR**	.05	.2	8	334	28.60	+ 0.15
6.50	3.06	LTC Prop **LTC**	j	. . .	dd*	550	6.00	. . .
98.07	60.70	L 3Comm **LLL**		. . .	31	7978	83.38	+ 0.43
6.24	2.19	LaQuintaProp **LQI**	.46j	. . .	dd	2198	5.11	− 0.09
21.80	14.19	LaZ Boy **LZB**	.36		30	1328	21.00	− 0.05
51.45	19.11	LaBranche **LAB**		. . .	24	3165	31.25	+ 0.73
1.4	25.48	LacledeGrp **LG**	1.34		15	243	23.70	− 1.10
39.08	19.38	LafargeNoAm **LAF**	.60		13	1796	36.63	+ 0.13
50.45	23.20	LandAmFnl **LFG**	.20	.8	dd	1806	24.50	
49.88	31.04	Lennar **LEN**	.05	.1	7	21648		+ 1.20

NOTE: dd indicates that the company had no profits for the year.

12. What did LNR close at yesterday?

13. Put the following stocks in order from least volatile to most volatile: LLL, LQI, LZB, LAB, and LG.

14. Of the following stocks, which two are the most favorable to purchase immediately: LTC, LZB, LAB, and LFG?

15. Calculate the yield percentage for the following stocks: LZB, LG, and LAF.

16. If LFG closed yesterday at $25, find the net change.

17. If LEN closed yesterday at $67.42, find the closing price.

PROJECTS

1. Choose a company on the New York Stock Exchange. By phone, mail, or email, order the company's 10K, or annual report. For the most current year, analyze the company's financial statement using ratio analysis. Compare trends and industry averages.

2. Choose any two companies who are natural competitors listed on the New York Stock Exchange. Order annual reports for both companies. Using ratio analysis, compare the two businesses. Which company's stock is a better value at the current market value?

3. You are planning to purchase an established retail business. The financial statement indicates a very healthy business, at least on paper. Using only the assets listed below, explain in detail the questions one should ask in analyzing the company's financial statement.

Proposed Retail Business
Current Assets:

Cash	$ 800,000
Marketable securities	$ 225,000
Accounts receivable	$1,821,000
Equipment	$ 130,000
Inventory	$3,142,000

PART THREE
Final Examinations

The examination and projects in Chapter 10 give you an opportunity to test all your retail mathematics skills. Any questions involving case studies use actual vendor's profitability reports, but the names of the retailers and manufacturers have been deleted for reasons of confidentiality.

In solving the questions, remember the following hints:

1. See through the haze. Seek only the numerical data necessary to answer the question.
2. Find the "sales goal." Every purchase has a sales contribution expectation.
3. Remember your key formulas:
   a. MMU = IMU − (MD × complement of IMU)
   b. Find sales goals by dividing the total retail purchases by the markdown percent converted to a decimal and added to the number "1."
4. Watch for discounts and other factors that can alter the gross margin.
5. Check your answers carefully.

EXERCISES

1. A retailer who works on an IMU of 54.5 percent and has a planned gross margin of 38 percent made a $200,000 purchase at retail from a coat manufacturer. At the end of the season, the purchase produced sales of $160,000. Do those sales equal or exceed the planned gross margin?

2. A retailer has the following departmental requirements:

    IMU = 52%

    Planned GM = 40%

    Retailer receives a 5% discount.

    The retailer placed an order for $48,500 at cost with vendor ABC. At the end of the selling season, vendor ABC's total sales were $80,834. Does the amount of sales generated by ABC satisfy the planned gross margin?

3. A retailer with an IMU of 51 percent has a planned markdown percent of 30 percent. This retailer is always granted a discount of 4 percent. An order is placed with vendor XYZ for $80,000 at retail. The vendor produced sales of $61,538.

   a. Find the actual gross margin percentage for vendor XYZ and

   b. compare planned to actual sales.

4. A children's department placed an order for $120,000 at retail from a vendor. The buyer expressed a desire for this vendor to conform to a required gross margin of 39 percent. The department works on an IMU of 50 percent. What should be the sales goal?

5. After reviewing data sent by a client, a Florida-based men's shirt manufacturer called the retailer and asked for help in determining the markdown and gross margin percentage. The retailer responded that all the necessary data for such calculations had been provided. The data provided is as follows:

$$\text{Net sales} = \$80,000$$
$$\text{CMS} \quad = \$45,000$$
$$\text{IMU} \quad = 56\%$$

Determine if the retailer is correct. Using this information, can you find the:

a. Markdown percentage

b. Gross margin percentage

6. A retailer was reviewing the following chart in anticipation of presenting the data to the manufacturer from whom the purchase was made. Review the data in the chart and validate or invalidate it.

Purchases at cost	$160,000
Planned MD %	30%
Actual MD %	35%
Planned MMU %	37.6%
Actual MMU %	35.2%
Department IMU %	52%
Actual sales	$246,913
Planned sales	$256,410
Difference	$ 9,497

7. A retail chain's men's furnishings department has the following goals:

IMU = 52%

PMD = 32%

Retail purchases of $170,000 of men's long-sleeved shirts were purchased from a Florida-based manufacturer. At the conclusion of the selling season, the shirt manufacturer had a gross margin of 38 percent. Did the shirt manufacturer's gross margin equal or exceed the retailer's plan?

8. An exclusive department store chain requires that its manufacturers reach a gross margin of 40 percent and offer a 6 percent discount to the retailer. Shortages of 3 percent will be subtracted from the gross margin percentage. This retailer has an IMU of 52.5 percent. One of the vendors, a dress manufacturer, posted the following figures:

Retail purchases = $200,000

Sales   = $152,000

Determine this manufacturer's gross margin percentage.

9. The sales manager for a shoe manufacturer receives the following data from a key retail account:

Shoe Manufacturer XYZ Profitability:

Actual gross margin = 32%

Retail purchases   = $160,000

Your retailer's goals are:

IMU   = 53%

Planned gross margin = 36%

The retailer is requesting markdown money in the amount of $8,000 for the gross margin deficit from the plan. Should the sales manager grant the markdown dollar request?

10. A retailer with an initial markup of 53 percent receives a 5 percent discount on all purchases. Adjust the IMU to include the discount.

11. A retailer, with an IMU of 52.5 percent, receives an 8 percent discount. Adjust the IMU to include the discount.

12. A buyer made a retail purchase totaling $142,000. The planned markdown percentage was 28; the actual markdown percentage was 31.5. Find the dollar differential between the two markdown percentages.

13. A department store buyer has an initial markup plan of 53 percent; her maintained markup goal is 38 percent. A purchase order is written for $84,000 at retail. What would her sales have to be to achieve her goal?

14. A retail buyer had the following figures:

    Net sales   = $110,500

    Cost of purchases = $65,500

    IMU   = 52%

    Find the markdown dollars.

15. A retailer purchases $63,000 at cost with an initial markup of 50.5 percent. Retail purchases will therefore be $127,273. The retailer received a 5 percent discount. After the season ended, the retailer achieved a total sales figure of $90,000.

    a.   Find the gross margin percentage without including the discount.

    b.   Find the gross margin percentage including the discount.

16. A retailer makes cost purchases of $150,000. The initial markup is 55 percent, so retail purchases should be $333,333. The retailer received a 3 percent discount. The total sales this retailer achieved was only $263,333.

    a. Find the actual gross margin percentage obtained including the discount.

    b. Once you obtain the actual GM percentage, use the maintained markup formula, with a discount-adjusted initial markup percentage, to prove your answer. (*Hint:* You will need to calculate the markdown percentage.)

Questions 17 through 19 are based on the following statement.

Company DEF
Income Statement in Millions

	2002
Net sales	76.67
Cost of goods sold	30.0
Gross profit	46.67
Operating expenses	40.0
Pretax profit	6.67
Taxes at 40%	2.67
Net income	4.0

Balance Sheet in Millions

	2002
Assets: Current cash	2.6
Accounts receivable	16.5
Inventory	29.5
Total current assets	48.0
Long-term assets building	34.0
Total assets	82.0
Liabilities: Current	6.0
Long term	4.0
Total liabilities	10.0
Stockholders equity	72.0
Common stock	
72,000 shares at $1 par value	
Total stockholders equity	72.0
Total liabilities and stockholders equity	82.0

---

17. Referring to Company DEF, solve the following ratios:

    a.   Current

    b.   Quick

    c.   Current liabilities to net worth

    d.   Net worth

    e.   Debt ratio

    f.   Profit margin

    g.   Gross profit margin

    h.   Return on total assets

    i.   Book value per share

    j.   Earnings per share

    k.   Price/earnings multiple (use current market value of $11 per share)

18. Compare the ratio solutions for Company DEF with industry standards. Compare only the following ratios:

    a.   Current ratio

    b.   Debt ratio

    c.   Profit margin

    d.   Return on total assets

19. Based upon the stock market ratio solutions, is company DEF's stock over- or undervalued?

20. Answer the following:

a. Complete the following profit-and-loss statement.

Net sales	$450,000
− CMS	_____
Gross margin $	$
Gross margin %	40%
Gross margin $	$
− Operating expenses	_____
PL $	$
P/L %	− 3%

b. Below is an unfinished profit-and-loss statement. If the company below is in the 40 percent income tax bracket and has paid interest of $100,000, complete the entire P/L statement.

Net sales	$4,000,000
− CMS	
Gross margin	$3,000,000
Operating expenses	45%
P/L	
Interest	
Pretax profit	
Tax	
Net income	

21. A dress department has a six-month turn plan of 1.75. In addition it has planned sales of $600,000. Answer the following:

 a.   What is the average inventory?

 b.   What is the monthly sales average?

 c.   What is the monthly turn average?

22. A women's shoe store has an average stock level of $100,000. The store has a weekly turn of 10 percent. Answer the following:

 a.   What is the six-month plan of turn?

 b.   What is the six-month sales plan?

23. If a retail store has an initial markup of 53 percent and markdowns of 27 percent, find the maintained markup.

24. An invoice was dated 6/10/02, with terms of 8/10 EOM. For a store to receive the discount, what is the latest date on which payment can be made?

25. Use the following information to find the turn for the month of June:

BOM Stock = $ 82,000

EOM Stock = $118,000

Sales   = $ 25,000

PROJECTS

1. Order the 10K report of a company included in the Dow for the past two years. Compare the years by using the key ratios. Decide if the ratio has improved, stayed the same, or deteriorated from the previous year.

2. Write a dialogue between a buyer and a sales agent negotiating a retail profitability agreement. Assume both the retailer and manufacturer are entering into a mutually dependent situation, in which both parties are dependent on each other for continuing business in order to succeed. How would each side prepare an agreement for continued business, but still highlight certain precautionary measures?

3. For the following businesses, explain in detail how an increase in the turn might produce greater profits:
   a. airline
   b. dentist
   c. movie studio

4. Show the dynamics as a major retailer passes through the four possible stages of the buyer-vendor relationship. Consider the following in your answer:
   a. Does a good relationship have to end?
   b. How can events deteriorate so that the relationship becomes confrontational?
   c. Why might a relationship end in the first, second, or third stage?

5. Pretend to create your own stock portfolio by starting with $10,000. Chart your progress over a six-month period, explaining your reasons for purchasing and selling specific stocks. Then, check your capital gains or losses for that period. Remember that a stock never has a capital gain or loss until you sell it.

Glossary

Accounts payable Legal debts a company must pay.

Accounts receivable All money owed to a company for product and services.

Accrued expenses Operational expenses that accrue for a short period of time before payment is made, such as salaries.

Additional markup Adjustment that increases the price of merchandise already in stock.

Average retail price Price that will achieve desired markup percentage.

Average retail stock The average amount of inventory at the beginning and end of each selling period.

Averaging markups The adjustment of the proportion of goods purchased at different markups.

Averaging retails The proportioning of different retail prices on purchases that have more than one cost to achieve the desired markup percentage.

Billed cost The manufacturer's price for goods offered to a retailer.

BOM stock The value of stock at the beginning of a month.

Bonds Instruments purchased that promise quarterly payment of interest for the life of the bond, as well as face value at maturity.

Cash on hand This is liquid funds available for immediate use.

Charge back Form on which the retailer notes a deduction to be taken from the manufacturer.

Closeout Goods, often a broken assortment, offered to the retailer at a reduced price.

Closing inventory The value of merchandise in stock at the end of an accounting period.

COD (cash on delivery) dating A form of payment in which the vendor requires full payment of the invoice when the merchandise is delivered.

Complement The difference between 100 and any number less than 100 (for example, the complement of 60 is 40).

Cost The amount a retailer pays a manufacturer for purchases.

Cost of goods sold The cost of merchandise that has been sold during a given period.

Cumulative markup The markup percentage achieved on all goods available for sale during a given period.

Dating An agreement specifying payment terms.

Discount date The date by which an invoice must be paid to take advantage of the discount granted.

Dividends Quarterly payments to holders of preferred and common stock, if such dividends are indicated.

Earnings or net income Income less expenses; it represents actual profits.

Employee discounts A percentage deduced from the regular retail price as a courtesy to employees of a retail organization.

EOM (end of month) dating A form of dating involving two different payment schedules depending on the day of the month on the invoice; the first is for invoices dated from the 1st to the 24th of a month; the second for invoices dated from the 25th until the last date of the month.

Equity The net worth of a business determined by deducting liabilities from assets.

Extra dating A form of dating that allows extra time for a retailer to pay an invoice by either the discount or net date.

Final selling price Price received when an item is sold.

FOB (free on board; freight on board) These terms establish both the legal transfer of ownership of the goods from the manufacturer to the retailer and also the point at which the retailer pays the cost of freight.

FOB factory The retailer owns the goods and pays for the freight at the point of shipment from the vendor.

FOB store This specifies that the manufacturer pays all freight and has full ownership of the merchandise until delivery to the retailer.

Gross margin (GM) The remainder after subtracting the total cost of goods sold from the total retail amount of sales; the difference between net sales and the cost of goods sold; also called gross profit.

Gross margin return per dollar of inventory (GMROI) The relationship between the average inventory at cost and gross margin; gross margin divided by average inventory at cost.

Gross markdown Original price reduction.

Gross sales Retail value of total initial sales before the deduction of the dollar amount returned by customers.

Initial markup percentage (IMU) The difference between the cost of goods and the original retail price; the first price placed on merchandise for resale, planned markups specified on orders for merchandise; a projected markup goal.

Inventory To a manufacturer, inventory means a finished product and the raw materials needed to produce it. To a retailer, inventory means merchandise, which can also be known as "stock," or "goods."

Invoice A bill presented by a vendor to a retailer for goods purchased.

List price A theoretical retail price set by manufacturers.

Loading   Intentionally increasing the amount of an invoice to a price that would allow theoretically greater cash discounts, but results in paying the net amount that the vendor quotes.

Maintained markup (MMU)   The difference between the cost of goods and the actual selling price of the merchandise sold.

Markdown (MD)   A reduction in the retail price; the difference between the original or present retail price and the new retail price; taken in dollars, but can be expressed as a percentage.

Markdown allowance   A monetary fine imposed on a manufacturer when the product sold to a retailer does not meet predetermined parameters of consumer acceptance and purchases.

Markdown percentage   Markdown expressed as a percentage of net sales.

Markup (MU)   The difference between cost and retail price expressed either in dollars or as a percentage.

Merchandise (Mds)   Stock or goods.

Net   What remains when nothing is left to deduct.

Net cost   No additional discounts are earned on merchandise purchased.

Net loss   When the operating expenses exceed the gross margin.

Net payment   Terms of sale that mean no discounts may be taken.

Net payment date   The date by which an invoice must be paid to maintain a favorable credit rating and avoid penalties.

Net profit   The difference between gross margin and operating expenses.

Net sales   The sales total after customer returns and allowances have been deducted from gross sales.

Notes and loans   Debts that can be both short and long-term (more than one year); debts that a company pays off in a monthly payment of interest and principal.

Open to buy (OTB)   The amount of unspent money available for purchasing merchandise.

Opening book inventory   The value of merchandise in stock at the beginning of an accounting period.

Opening inventory   The retail value of merchandise in stock.

Operating expenses   Disbursals incurred in running an organization.

Overage   Dollar difference between the book stock figure and the physical count when the latter is the larger of the two.

Physical inventory   The retail dollar value of all goods physically present in a periodic stock count.

Planned markdown (PMD)   The reduction in retail price that was anticipated.

Planned purchases   The dollar amount of merchandise that can be bought into a stock during a given period.

Prepaid   Payment of transportation charges by the vendor when merchandise is shipped.

Profit   The dollar amount remaining after costs and expenses are paid.

Profit-and-loss (P/L) statement   Statement prepared periodically that summarizes the basic merchandising factors that affect profitability.

Purchase order   A formal document for merchandise from a retail store to a manufacturer.

Purchase order violations   Condition in which the manufacturer did not follow the instructions on the retailer's purchase order.

Regular dating   Discount date calculated from the date of an invoice.

Retailer   Any store that purchases product to sell at a profit.

Retailing   The act of selling to the customer or consumer.

Retail price   The price at which goods are sold to the ultimate consumer.

Retail reductions   Markdowns, stock shortages, and employee discounts.

Revenues   Sales dollars earned by a company. Revenues do not indicate profits.

ROG (receipt of goods) dating   A form of dating that changes the payment due date from the date on the invoice to the date on which the retailer received the merchandise.

Routing violations   Condition in which the manufacturer did not follow the retailer's request as to the method of shipping merchandise.

Sales volume   Dollar value of merchandise sold.

Shortage   Dollar difference between the book stock figure and physical count figures, when the former is the larger of the two.

Solvency   Solvency is the ability of a business to meet its debt. In addition to meeting debt, a company is solvent when the assets exceed liabilities (debts) by a comfortable margin.

Stock   An ownership share in a corporation, or an accumulation of merchandise.

Stockholder's equity   The value of assets minus liabilities.

Stock-sales ratio   The proportion between the BOM stock figure and the dollar amount of sales for the same month.

Stock turnover   The selling or turning over of inventory.

Terms of sale   Arrangement between a vendor and retailer relative to time period of invoice, cost of merchandise, shipping charges, and transportation arrangements.

Total cost of goods   Combines the cost of merchandise purchased and inward transportation costs.

Total cost of goods sold The amount obtained by subtracting cash discounts and adding workroom costs to the gross cost of merchandise sold; the total merchandise handled less the cost of the closing inventory.

Total merchandise handled (TMH) The sum of the opening inventory plus the total retail value of purchases that constitutes all merchandise available for sale.

Turn The number of times at which the average retail stock has been sold and replaced within a specified sales period.

Vendor A merchandise source, such as a manufacturer or distributor.

Vendor analysis An investigation of the profitability of each vendor's products sold by a retailer.

Volume The retail value of sales for a given period, usually expressed annually.

Workroom costs Charges for putting merchandise into condition for sale, such as assembling and polishing.

Answers to Odd-Numbered Exercises

CHAPTER 1

Types of Relationships

1. In a perfect world, the vendor and the buyer would each push to increase profits. In such a case, the progression from stage 1 to stage 3 would be smooth and mutually profitable. The perfect stage to achieve is one of mutual dependency. Unfortunately, too often the relationship becomes confrontational—and a breakdown in business occurs.

3. If a retailer risks a large purchase from a vendor, the entire success of the season may require the financial reimbursement provided by a profitability contract.

5. No

7. April 10

9. 30 days to pay with no discount

11. Payment is made at the time the retailer receives the merchandise.

13. It lowers the cost of the merchandise sold.

CHAPTER 2

Deals: The Intricacies of Partnership

1. A store or department often projects a desired gross margin that is unrealistic and unobtainable. The retailer does this to hold the manufacturer to a profit that guarantees a profitable gross margin. The actual gross margin is the true measure of profitability for the time in question.

3. The manufacturer should check with the buyer to make certain the payment has not been put on "hold." Only the buyer or the buyer's supervisor can remove the hold payment order.

5. Gross margin is important because it produces profits or losses.

7. The retailer received $11,000.

9. The manufacturer should not send a check; the retailer should deduct the amount from its purchases.

11. The manufacturer should take into consideration the unpredictability of the weather. If there is no snow, the retailer will have a poor sales season and produce a low gross margin. The manufacturer might find itself responsible for the losses.

CHAPTER 3

Vendor Analysis: Measuring Profitability

1. Maintained markup = 39.84%

3. Markdown = 27.47%

5. Sales = $64,615; markdowns = $19,385

7. Difference = $1,770

9. Difference = $10,687

11. 25%

13. $\dfrac{\text{BOM} + \text{EOM}}{2} = \dfrac{106,000 + 92,000}{2} = 99,000$

CHAPTER 4

Retailer's Report Card

1. a. GM = 30%

   b. GM = 33.5%

3. a. GM = 45%

   b. Student should double check answer in part (a).

5.

Vendor	Cost spent	Retail sales	GM%	% of OTB	% of sales
A	30,000	50,000	40%	7.3%	8%
B	110,000	170,000	35.3%	26.8%	27.2%
C	40,000	50,000	20%	9.75	8%
D	20,000	36,000	44.4%	4.9%	5.8%
E	150,000	210,000	28.6%	36.6%	33.5%
F	60,000	110,000	45.5%	14.6%	17.6%
Total	410,000	626,000	34.5%		

7. a. MD = 32%

   b. IMU = 52%

   c. Actual cost = $203,700

9. MD = 25%

11. Retail purchase = $96,154

13. No. The retailer did not credit the manufacturer with the 8 percent discount.

CHAPTER 5

Negotiation

1. The tactics should include discussions of employee discounts, shortages, and workroom costs. These deductions resulted in the deficit GM%.

3. The manufacturer should never write a check. The request could mean that the retailer does not plan on any future purchases from the manufacturer.

5. The manufacturer should "push the business" (that is, increase its volume with the retailer).

7. & 9. In addition to performing the mathematical calculation to determine gross margin dollar difference, the students should use the various negotiating options discussed in this chapter.

11. Students should explain the moral, ethical, business, and legal ramifications.

CHAPTER 6

Turn: The Life and Breath of Retail

1. Sales = $85,500

3. Weekly turn = 0.077

5. Sales = $300,000

7. Monthly sales level = $75,000

9. a. Average turn per night = 2

   b. The income will increase by $1,800 from $3,600 to $5,400.

11. The monthly turn should exceed the six-month plan.

CHAPTER 7

Retail versus Cost Method of Markup

1. 150%

3. 89.5%

5. 58.33%

7. 51.8% or 51.9%

9. 42.86%

11. 48.72%

13. 92.3%

15. 111%

CHAPTER 8

Profit-and-Loss Statements

1. CMS = $200,000

   OPX = $160,000

3. CMS = $215,800

   GM = $199,200

   OPX = $186,750

   P/L = [− $12,450]

5. a. Loss

   b. Loss: 2%

7. Net earnings = $900,000

9. Operating expenses = 40%

11. Gross margin = 47%

13. Cost of merchandise sold = 55%

CHAPTER 9

Balance Sheets

1. See chart in answer manual.

3. Yes, the stock lost 73 percent of its value.

5. Company GHI's stock is much less volatile. GHI had a 34 percent loss compared to a 75 percent loss for DEF.

7. Closing price = $18.88

9. Closing price = $61.37

11. a. GHI   1.7%

     b. MNO   1.3%

     c. STU   1.3%

13. Most volatile to least volatile:

LQI	65%
LAB	63%
LLL	38%
LZB	35%
LG	16.6%

15. Yield percentages:

LZB = 1.7%

LG = 5.7%

LAF = 1.6%

17. Closing price: $68.62

CHAPTER 10

Exercises and Projects

1. Actual sales exceeded the gross margin plan.

3. a. Actual gross margin = 38.9%

     b. Actual and planned sales were the same.

5. a. Markdown   = 27.8%

     b. Gross margin = 43.8%

7. The actual gross margin of 38 percent exceeded the planned gross margin percentage.

9. No. The request exceeds the true difference in sales.

11. Adjusted IMU = 56.3%

13. Sales = $63,685

15. a. Gross margin = 30%

    b. Gross margin = 33.5%

17. a. Current = 8

    b. Quick = 3.08

    c. Current liabilities to net worth = 8%

    d. Net worth = $72 million

    e. Debt ratio = 12%

    f. Profit margin = 5.2%

    g. Gross profit margin = 61%

    h. Return on total assets = 4.9%

    i. Book value per share = $1,000

    j. Earnings per share = $55.6

    k. Price/earnings multiple = 20

19. The stock is undervalued.

21. a. Average inventory = $342,857

    b. Monthly sales average = $100,000

    c. Monthly turn average = 0.29

23. Maintained markup = 40.31%

25. Turn = 0.25

Index

manufacturer, buyer and, 3
    See also buyer-vendor relationships;
        negotiations
manufacturer's label, 80
markdown dollars, 40, 65
markdown (MD), 19, 59–60
    negotiation of, 80, 87
    point of sale, 60
markdown (MD) allowance, 5, 25, 26
    negotiation of, 80, 81, 83–84, 85, 88
    seasonal analysis of, 42, 43, 50
markdown percentage, 35, 44
    expected sales and, 37–39, 40
    in monthly flow chart, 48
    in profitability report, 43, 64, 65
markdown requests, 47–48. *See also*
        markdown allowance
marketable securities, 144
market value, stock, 154, 157
market week, 81
markup (MU), 25, 66
    negotiation of, 84, 85
markup (MU) methods, 1
    See also cost *vs.* retail method of
        markup; initial markup
        percentage; maintained
        markup
MD. *See* markdown
merchandise (Mds.), 1
    cost of, 8, 19, 65
    off-price, 21
    return policies, 4, 5, 21, 26, 83
    total handled (TMH), 46
merchandise turnover. *See* turn (turn
       rate)
merchandising, turn and, 102
MMU. *See* maintained markup (MMU)
monthly flow chart, 41, 45–50, 70
MU. *See* markup
mutual need, 6

negotiations, 79–96
    See also deals, partnership and
    buyer-vendor, 1, 4, 6–7, 8
    contract, 23–26, 81
    "King's Gambit," 88

manufacturer's lament, 87
markdown requests in, 80, 83–84
with no retailer-manufacturer
    guarantee, 81–85
profitability reports and, 84, 87,
    95–96
renegotiating a pre-existing deal,
    87–88
retailer-vendor partnership and,
    85–86
net payment, 8
net payment date, 8, 26
net profit, 151
net sales, gross margin and, 19, 25
net worth, 142
    of inventory, 145
net worth formula, 149–150
net worth ratio formula, 143
new accounts, 4
New York Stock Exchange, 155, 171
notes and loans, 141, 146

off-price merchandise, 21
online retailing, 118
open to buy (OTB), 31, 61–62, 63
operating expenses (OPX), 19, 129, 130
    online retailing and, 118
operating statement, 129
OPX. *See* operating expenses
OTB. *See* open to buy (OTB)
over-the-counter tables, 158
owners' equity, 142
ownership
    corporate shares, 131
    of merchandise, 9

partnerships, 48
    See also deals, partnership and
    retailer-vendor, 85–86
payment
    end-of-season, 86
    holdup of, 22, 81
    net, 8
PE. *See* price/earnings (PE) multiple
performance analysis, 41. *See also*
    seasonal analysis

physical inventory, 36
P/L. *See* profit and loss
planned markdown (PMD), 37, 40
point goal, 23
point of sale markdown, 60
price, discounts and, 43
price, line, 65
price/earnings (PE) multiple, 155,
    157–158
price/earnings (PE) ratio, 157–158, 159
production prototype, 36
profit, 1
profitability
    buyer-vendor relationship and, 1,
        3–4, 6
    contracts for, 5, 24
    expected sales and, 36–40
    gross margin and, 19, 130
    guaranteed, 24
    measuring, 35–57
    mutual, 25
    seasonal analysis of, 41–45, 50
    turn rate as measure of, 97,
        102–103
profitability formulas, 151–153
profitability margin, 151
profitability reports, 59
    See also retailer's report card
    analysis of, 64–65
    negotiation and, 84, 87, 95–96
profit-and-loss (P/L) statement, 35,
    129–139
    components of, 129
    evaluating, 129–131
purchase orders
    cancellation of, 17
    dating provisions for, 8
    violations, 5, 7, 25–26
purchasing plans, 50

quality control, 26, 36
quick ratio, 147, 149

ratio analysis, of financial statements,
    146–151
receipt of goods (ROG), 8